LEAN IS NOT MEAN

68 Practical Lessons in Lean Leadership

Bob Emiliani

The CLBM, LLC
Wethersfield, Conn.

Lean Is Not Mean: 68 Practical Lessons in Lean Leadership / M.L. "Bob" Emiliani

ISBN-13: 978-0-9898631-3-1

Library of Congress Control Number: 2015909610

1. Leadership 2. Business 3. Lean Management
4. Management 5. Organizations

First Edition: June 2015

Published previously as e-books titled: *Kaizen Heart and Mind: A Collection of Insightful Essays on Lean Leadership*, Volume 1 (2011), Volume 2 (2012), Volume 3 (2014), and *Lean IS Healthcare* (2012). This print version is revised and expanded.

Published by The CLBM, LLC, Wethersfield, Connecticut, USA

Manufactured using digital print-on-demand technology.

For Michael and Julia.

See Things Differently

CONTENTS

CONTENTS

CONTENTS

Preface

The long-term viability of Lean as an alternative management system depends on the ability of its practitioners to recognize the differences, both great and small, between it and conventional management practice.

Foremost among the differences is the way in which Lean management must be led. For some three decades, the great majority of leaders have led Lean in ways that resulted in good outcomes for the company and its shareholders, but bad outcomes for employees, suppliers, and other key stakeholders.

If it's mean, it's not Lean.

The intent of Lean management is to create outcomes that are good for everyone: employees, suppliers, customers, investors, and communities.

This book will help leaders close the gap between actual outcomes and required outcomes. It presents 68 practical lessons to improve their understanding and practice of Lean management and achieve outcomes that benefit all stakeholders.

Lean is a progressive, human-centered system of management. It evolved over the decades in response human and economic needs to create better experiences for all key stakeholders – not worse experiences. The harm to people caused by the incorrect understanding and practice of Lean management has long been a concern of mine. Managers at all levels think Lean management is easy to understand and practice. This is a big mistake. Learning Lean management is more like learning to play piano well than learning how to ride a bicycle.

Executives, in particular, confuse a little bit of Lean knowledge with deep understanding of Lean derived from actual Lean practice. As a result, they make dozens of fundamental errors that cause harm to the community of stakeholders – the people who are needed in order for a business to function effectively.

In Lean, a primary objective is to improve processes to get material and information to flow without interruption. Misunderstanding and misapplying Lean principles and practices means that this important objective cannot be achieved.

The zero-sum (win-lose) thinking and outcomes that are the staple of conventional management practice are transferred to Lean management practice. This must ever happen, but it does. Executives, not knowing any better, set people up to fail in their zero-sum practice of Lean management and drive people away from continuous improvement activities.

Please know this: It ceases to be Lean management the moment it is used for bad.

Instead, executives must understand and practice Lean as intended: a non-zero-sum (win-win) management system. They must attract people and develop their desire to participate in daily continuous improvement. This, it turns out, has proven over time to be enormously difficult, as executives are more likely to continue doing what made them successful and ignore anything that requires them to learn something both new and substantial.

My focus since the mid-1990s has been to teach managers how to cross this chasm by teaching them Lean leadership and by making the "Respect for People" principle come alive. This book, as well as my other books, seeks to deepen leaders' understanding of both Lean management and Lean leadership. The information contained in this book will make you think and help you become a better leader.

Organizations that practice Lean well will be better positioned to compete globally. In addition to enjoying improved financial and non-financial performance, work becomes more fun for employees and managers, and all other stakeholders. Everyone must benefit from Lean management.

My purpose is to advance REAL Lean thinking and practice worldwide, not only for its business benefits, but also to elevate humanity and alleviate human suffering. Leadership and work must proceed in this direction.

My vision is that people leave work every day healthier, both physically and mentally, than when they arrived. You should adopt this vision as well. To make it become reality, leaders have to recognize that much of their daily activity is in service of abnormal conditions. They must recognize this, determine the normal condition, and strive to achieve it. At the same time, they must create large blocks of time in their schedule to develop people with the company and interact with outside stakeholders to improve relations.

Your time on earth is precious. I hope this book helps you in your effort to become a capable Lean leader and do many good things.

Bob Emiliani
June 2015
Wethersfield, Conn.

Introduction

Executives driven to become effective Lean leaders become changed persons – changed for the better, for both self and for others. Everything must change not only with respect to the business, but also the way leaders see things, think about things, and the way they do things.

They experience a personal transformation that comes from accumulated Lean practice and learning. What they once saw as "good enough" or "that's just the way things are" – abnormal conditions – they now see as having unlimited potential for improvement striving towards the normal condition.

Their commitment, sense of curiosity, and passion for improvement drives them to learn even more and to continue deepening their understanding of Lean management.

It is difficult to describe in words effective Lean leaders' commitment, curiosity, and passion for improvement. Think of it as a chronic hunger that must be satisfied with great urgency, but which is never truly satisfied. They have boundless energy and enjoy every aspect of their work, and they dig into the details in ways that you have probably never done before.

To get a better sense of this, watch the documentary movie *Jiro Dreams of Sushi* and the PBS television show *The Mind of a Chef*. You will learn much from people who have deeply committed themselves to improving their trade every day, and, as a result, have created something truly special that they continue to build upon. I am sure you will find it inspiring.

Watch these videos over and over again with discerning eyes and ears. Study them. Take notes as you watch. Capture the attitude and mindset of the chefs, what they say, and the level of detail they work to. Study your notes to more deeply comprehend their meaning. Then, translate what you learn to your environment.

I am certain that, if you are honest, you will see your company as more similar to a haphazardly run diner than a Michelin-rated restaurant. Take the time to learn from these videos and other resources to lead your company's Lean transformation.

You may ask: "Why is Lean important to an organization?" or "Why should I introduce Lean to an organization that already has good performance?" These are good questions. Most of the writing about Lean focuses on organizations that perform poorly and need to improve.

Lean is important to an organization to help it survive for the long-term, as it faces new competition and changing macroeconomic conditions. Lean, done right, makes an organization more flexible and adaptable to change as it occurs (rather than delayed responses). Survival gives an organization the continuing opportunity to serve its customers over time and to meet their increasingly challenging demands.

Leaders should introduce Lean to an organization with good performance because good performance is relative. Most organizations process material information using the batch-and-queue method (an abnormal condition). If that is all you compete against, then performance can appear to be good – despite having many unhappy customers. Customer expectations go in one direction over time: up. If we are truly customer focused, then the reason we practice Lean is to better satisfy customers, continuously, over time.

But, there is more to it than that. Lean management is a better way to contend with low economic growth, which we may face for some time to come. Process improvement pays for things that an organization needs or what it must do for its stakeholders. The payoff will be low and slow if leaders fail to recognize Lean as a solution to information flow problems, and which also has the knock-on effect of improving human health in organizations.

For an organization to reap the benefits of Lean, leaders have to admit all work processes can be improved, and that nobody is exempt from improvement. An organization where everyone improves their work processes, top to bottom, in non-zero-sum (win-win) ways, is one that progresses and will survive and prosper for the long-term. Continuous flow is the normal condition for all processes, and that is what leaders should strive to achieve.

When you think about the core attributes of Lean management (i.e. Toyota's management method), one cannot help but to be impressed:

- Lean is pragmatic - reality and fact-based.
- Lean improves communication, cooperation, and enthusiasm for work throughout the enterprise.
- Lean offers tangible opportunities for everyone to contribute in meaningful ways every day.
- Problem-solving is localized, rather than centralized in the executive suite.
- Lean is fiscally responsible (cash-rich vs. debt-poor).
- Lean grows the economic pie, instead of stakeholders fighting over the size of their slice (behavioral waste).
- There is no better way to lead or manage a business that is engaged in free markets.
- Eliminating waste, unevenness, and unreasonableness is like cutting taxes. Who doesn't like lower taxes?
- Lean contributes to good stewardship of Earth's resources in ways that are mostly free.
- Lean results in greater prosperity.
- Lean, done well, makes you exceptional.

Lean is great friend to labor and capital alike. Both must recognize this.

There is more. Lean management - understood and practiced correctly - functions as an intelligent safety system. It helps organizations avoid nasty collisions with other stakeholders: customers, employees, suppliers, investors, communities, and even competitors. How does it do that?

- Lean helps you avoid over-production and under-production.
- Lean (flow) helps you maintain low costs on a continuing basis.
- Lean improves information flow, so you get fewer nasty surprises.
- People trained in Lean can more quickly recognize problems and correct problems, and do so better and less expensively.
- There are fewer and less severe quality problems, and are they recognized earlier in the process.
- Lean businesses are not on defense when it comes to profits; they are on offense and thus consistently more profitable.

LSS is actually an abbreviation for "Lean Safety System," not Lean Six Sigma.

Lean management works for any business and industry. The challenge, of course, is for everyone - CEO on down - to learn Lean through the daily application of its principles and practices, to improve the management system so that its many benefits grow over time. There will be a further challenge to assure continuity of Lean practice through changes in management and changes in ownership.

Lesson 1

The Equally Important "Respect for People" Principle

The "Respect for People" principle is one of two pillars of The Toyota Way [1]; the other is "Continuous Improvement." The "Respect for People" principle has existed for several decades within Toyota's management system, but has been almost entirely ignored by outsiders until recently. This principle extends back to the 1900s and was recognized as essential by the creators of the Scientific Management system [2] – of which Lean management is its direct descendent [3] in tandem with Ford's flow production system. In the old days, the "Respect for People" principle was referred to more narrowly as "Cooperation," principally between management and labor [4, 5], because that was the pressing issue of the day.

As many people have found out firsthand, practicing only the "Continuous Improvement" principle (called "Betterment" in the old days [2, 5]) leads to many problems. Foremost among them is management's desire to improve efficiency and productivity usually results in layoffs, which slows down or halts improvement efforts. Root cause analyses of the problems that arise when only the "Continuous Improvement" principle is practiced indicates a countermeasure that today we call the "Respect for People" principle [3]. This point is worth repeating: "Respect for People" (Cooperation) is the primary countermeasure for bungled continuous improvement (Betterment) efforts. That's why it is a Toyota Way principle.

Indeed, the failure of the Scientific Management system to firmly establish itself in industry 60-100 years ago was correctly attributed to management's inability to establish long-term patterns of cooperative and respectful behavior with labor, in addition to other leadership shortcomings [6]. The same thing is happening today. Lean management is struggling to replace conventional management on a narrow basis, let alone across wide swaths of manufacturing and service industries. It should be no surprise that history is repeating itself.

The "Respect for People" principle is deceptive in that it seems very easy to understand and apply, but it is not. Most mid- and senior-level managers think they know what "Respect for People" means, but it is clear from leadership behaviors, common business performance metrics, company policies, management's decisions, and sometimes even corporate strategy, that they do not.

Top managers typically possess superficial, casual definitions of "Respect for People" such as fairness, civility, or listening. And they think they do these things quite well. Further, they think understanding the meaning of "Respect for People" is trivial for well-educated persons in high positions. This is a severe misjudgment. Far from being trivial, it is of great importance to the long-term survival and prosperity of a business to understand what "Respect for People" really means.

Toyota does not use one simple, discrete definition to express the "Respect for People" principle. Its context is better represented by the phrase "Respect for Stakeholders" in a narrow context [1] and also humanity in a larger context [7]. Rather, it is a more elaborate multi-layered description that includes historical words from former Toyota executives to better comprehend its meaning. Toyota's top-level representation of the "Respect for People" principle consists of two parts: "Respect" and "Teamwork," and is as follows [1, 8]:

> "RESPECT: We respect others, make every effort to understand each other, take responsibility and do our best to build mutual trust.
>
> TEAMWORK: We stimulate personal and professional growth, share the opportunities of

> development and maximize individual and team performance."

These words do not constitute the entire definition. A significant amount of detail is missing and can be found only in the "The Toyota Way 2001" document [1], which is not publicly available. But don't fall into the trap of hoping to obtain a copy of the document. Instead, please start to think about what "Respect for People" means in the context of stakeholders, corporate policies, metrics, business processes, leadership behaviors, corporate strategy, etc.

While the Toyota Way 2001 document does much to reduce variation in individual perceptions of what the equally important "Continuous Improvement" and "Respect for People" principles mean, words printed on paper are never sufficient. The "Respect for People" principle is comprehended only through daily thinking and practice on-the-job. It requires years of thought and practice to understand it well, and can never be completely comprehended.

James Womack, founder and chairman of the Lean Enterprise Institute, sent an e-mail note to the Lean community titled "Respect for People" [9]. In it, he spoke of this principle in the context of the manager-associate dyad, which is what most people think of when they hear about the "Respect for People" principle. While this is a very important dyad, it is not the only relationship that matters.

The "Respect for People" principle encompasses all key stakeholders: employees, suppliers, customers, investors, and communities [1, 10]. Thus, rather than representing a single dyad, the "Respect for People" principle is a multilateral expression of the need for balanced, mutually respectful relationships, cooperation, and co-prosperity with these key stakeholders. So in the context of Lean management, the "Respect for People" principle is anything but trivial to understand.

It is worthwhile now to briefly trace the origins and evolution of this principle to illustrate that it has been around for many decades, but only rarely has it been put into effective practice by senior managers. That's because their focus has long been the near-singular pursuit of productivity and efficiency improvements to lower costs and increase profits, usually culminating in layoffs – a zero-sum outcome for employees that violates the "Respect for People" principle.

In the late 1800s, leading business thinkers and doers began to press for improved cooperation between labor and management to overcome systemic strife between these two parties. They did this for practical reasons, not theoretical ones. Poor cooperation increased costs, and these costs could be avoided. Today we would say: leadership behaviors that foment conflict are waste because they add cost but do not add value and can be eliminated [11].

R.W. Cooke-Taylor, the author of *Modern Factory System* [4] published in 1891, said:

> "Among reflections recently made was the disappointing one of the strained relations often existing under the modern factory system between employers and employed. Some grave dangers were pointed out which the future may have in store for us in this connection, and the inconveniences of the situation must be patent to everyone. The cure most usually proposed… is that of co-operation."

In this quote, "co-operation" means a business is operated jointly by labor and management, as "part proprietors," with profit-sharing, to "ameliorate the rivalries of capital and labor… [which] affects large savings in the cost of production." In other words, eliminating wasteful labor-management rivalries reduces costs. However, we must not forget that wasteful rivalries can exist among other stakeholders such as suppliers, investors, and even customers, which also increase costs.

Soon thereafter "cooperation" took on a meaning in business that we are more familiar with: working together to satisfy common interests. In his 1903 paper titled "Shop Management," Frederick Taylor stressed the importance of cooperation and respect for people in the following ways [5]:

> "First, then, the men must be brought to see that the new system changes their employers from antagonists to friends who are working as hard as possible, side by side with them, all pushing in the same direction…"

> "In making this decision [to reorganize], as in taking each subsequent step, the most important consideration, which should always be first in the mind of the reformer, is 'what effect will this step have upon the workman'?"

> "The mistake that ninety-nine men [managers] out of a hundred make is that they have attempted to influence a large body of men at once [with major changes in the management system] instead of taking one man at a time."

The last quote is interesting because most senior managers today, just as they did in the early 1900s, impose change upon people in large batches, rather than one at a time. The latter approach recognizes employees as individuals whose concerns about changes in the management system are not uniform and can only be addressed by personal contact.

Frederick Taylor continued to stress the importance of cooperation and respect for people in his 1911 book, *The Principles of Scientific Management* [2]:

> "…almost every act of the workman should be preceded by one or more preparatory acts of the

> management which enable him to do his work better and quicker than he otherwise could."
>
> "They [management] heartily cooperate with the men so as to ensure all of the work is being done in accordance with the principles of the science which has been developed."

Taylor's most thorough explanation of the need for cooperation and respect for people is found in his testimony to Congress in 1912 [12].

That's the early view of cooperation and respect for people, which was seen as a practical necessity to reduce conflict and help achieve higher productivity, lower costs, and better quality.

So how could Lean practitioners have become familiar with the "Respect for People" principle prior to it coming to the forefront within the last few years? Well, it was hiding in plain view for decades; they would have found it to be a consistent theme in the writings and speeches of current and former Toyota executives, as well as some who have closely studied Toyota's management system. What follows are a few brief examples of where the "Respect for People" principle has appeared in various books and papers, arranged chronologically.

Shotaro Kamiya (d. 1980) was a past Chairman of Toyota Motor Sales. In his 1976 memoir *My Life With Toyota*, Kamiya refers to the "Respect for People" principle in terms of how automobile dealers are treated by automobile manufacturers [13] when he worked for General Motors (before joining Toyota, circa 1935):

> "Their [General Motors] policy toward dealers was especially merciless, and almost daily they cut ties with dealers in financial trouble. I remember thinking that while such action might be accepted business practice in the United States, where companies rely greatly on written contracts, customs are different in Japan and

> GM officers should try to understand the local situation more. I often complained to the American staff and tried to persuade them to help dealers instead of dropping them, especially since I visited dealers and knew firsthand their predicament. But GM ignored my complaints. It was at this time that I thought out one of my most important business principles, the necessity for coexistence and co-prosperity with dealers... my emphasis on respect for the dealer inspired many men from other companies to join Toyota."

Fujio Cho, the current Chairman of Toyota Motor Corporation, co-authored a paper in 1977 titled: "Toyota Production System and Kanban System: Materialization of Just-in-Time and Respect-for-Human System" [14]. The "Respect for Human" system was characterized as follows:

> "...the 'respect-for-human' system where the workers are allowed to display in full their capabilities through active participation in running and improving their own workshops... which is the most distinctive feature of Toyota's respect for human system."

> "Toyota firmly believes that making up a system where the capable Japanese workers can actively participate in running and improving their workshops and be able to fully display their capabilities would be [the] foundation of human respect environment of the highest order."

Toyota has profit sharing and associates who participate in operating the business. This sounds a lot like what R.W. Cook-Taylor said about "co-operation" in his 1891 book *Modern Factory System*. Here is another instructive quote from Mr. Cho's paper:

"It is not a conveyer that operates men, while it is men that operate a conveyer, which is the first step to respect for human independence."

One could say today: "It is not a computer [e.g. SAP] that operates men, while it is men that operate a computer, which is the first step to respect for human independence."

Seisi Kato, who followed Shotaro Kamiya as Chairman of Toyota Motor Sales, said the following in his 1981 memoir, *My Years With Toyota* [15], in relation to employees and dealers:

> "I adopted what I call the Three C's, standing for Communication, Consideration and Cooperation. What they signify is both a method of personal communication and a method of management. Handing down orders is not leadership, nor is issuing policies enough to constitute business relationships. In my view leadership is a process springing from dialogue that reaches the level of true communication, followed by sincere efforts at cooperation based upon mutual consideration and understanding of each other's position."

Professor Yasuhiro Monden's 1983 book *Toyota Production System: Practical Approach to Production Management*, states [16]:

> "…respect-for-humanity, [which allows] each worker to participate in the production process."

> "Respect for humanity: Since quality control based on autonomation calls immediate attention to defects or problems in the production process, it stimulates improvement activities and thus increases respect for humanity."

Taiichi Ohno, former Executive Vice President of Toyota Motor Corporation, said in the Preface of his 1988 book *Toyota Production System: Beyond Large-Scale Production* [17]:

> "The most important objective of the Toyota System has been to increase production efficiency by consistently and thoroughly eliminating waste. This concept and the equally important respect for humanity that has passed down from the venerable Toyoda Sakichi (1867-1930), founder of the company and master of inventions, to his son Toyoda Kiichiro (1894-1952), Toyota Motor Company's first president and father of the Japanese passenger car, are the foundations of the Toyota production system."

Note the words "equally important," which means the "Respect for People" principle is not optional, though most mangers seem to think it is optional. And note that "eliminating waste" (continuous improvement) and "respect for humanity" are "the foundations" of Toyota's production system – and Toyota's overall management system as well. Too bad many people don't bother reading the Preface of books, or when they do read these books they are too focused on Lean tools to notice the foundational principles.

Masaaki Imai, founder and chairman of the Kaizen Institute, made significant efforts to reinforce respect for people, cooperation, etc., in his 1987 book, *Kaizen: The Key to Japan's Competitive Success* [18], and in his popular late-1980s kaizen training seminars [19].

In 1991 Michael Husar, who was an assembly coordinator at NUMMI, the General Motors-Toyota joint venture in Fremont, Calif., wrote an internal company paper titled: "Corporate Culture: Toyota's Secret, Competitive Advantage" [20]. The paper presented in a very concise and efficient way the differences between GM and Toyota corporate culture. It was intended for GM management, who was Husar's employer at the joint venture, as a way to help promote needed changes in GM's corporate culture.

The paper, based largely on Toyota internal training (similar in many ways to "The Toyota Way 2001" document that appeared 10 years later), contained a section titled: "Respect for the Value of People." In it, Husar says:

> "Toyota believes its growth as a business enterprise comes through the growth of its people. This means to be successful, Toyota must utilize its employees' abilities as effectively as possible, and help each person develop the ability to think and execute the job more effectively
>
> Toyota has plants, equipment, and capital resources, but these things do not build cars. Its team members build the cars. Its team members also add value to its products by suggesting ways to improve their work and the production process. Toyota realizes that it is responsible for providing its employees the opportunity to contribute their ideas, as well as their labor.
>
> Toyota also believes that to get the best from its employees, it must respect their competence, and provide them with jobs that use and challenge their abilities. Toyota realizes the value of its people, and wants them to think of the company as a place where everyone can learn from one another, and grow as individuals, rather than just as a place to work."

Another section titled "Mutual Trust Between Employees and Management" says:

> "Mutual trust means that management and the employees have confidence in one another. Management and their employees have different jobs

> and different responsibilities in the company. Mutual trust comes from the belief that everyone is, however, striving for the same purpose...
>
> Toyota realizes this kind of mutual trust is not a given condition between management and the employees. It must be earned through many mutual efforts that create confidence.
>
> Toyota values and tries to maintain mutual trust, because it is the foundation for the growth of the company and its employees."

Yukiyasu Togo, another former Chairman of Toyota Motor Sales said in his 1997 memoir *Yuki Togo's Sell Like Hell!!* [21]:

> "For two people to develop trustworthy and respectful relationships they must meet each other face to face as often as possible. This makes possible the very best opportunity for good communications. They must also show consideration of one another's situation, feelings, and needs, and share a willingness to cooperate... Without good human relations, you cannot really grow or prosper, so the 'Three C's' are a vital part of any success formula."

In the award-winning 1998 paper, "Lean Behaviors," I coined the terms "Lean behaviors" and "behavioral waste" [11]. The paper identifies value-added leadership behaviors (respect is one of them) and leadership behaviors that are waste because they add cost but do not value and can be eliminated. It says:

> "The concept of 'lean' behaviors is analogous to lean production. Lean behaviors are defined simply as behaviors that add or create value. It is the minimization of waste associated with arbitrary or contradictory thoughts and actions that leads to

> defensive behavior, ineffective relationships, poor cooperation, and negative attitudes.
>
> In contrast, behaviors that inhibit work flow are analogous to wasteful batch and queue mass production methods. These behaviors are… defined as behaviors that add no value and can be eliminated. They include the display of irrational and confusing information that results in delays or work stoppages, or the articulation of unsubstantiated subjective thoughts and opinions.
>
> It is not inconceivable that someday investors, suppliers, customers, or employees will begin to question the cost or ethics of 'fat' behaviors in a manner similar to recent stakeholder concerns about a company's environmental record or their presence in countries that lack basic human rights. Critical stakeholders such as investors or employees may precipitate improved behaviors once they more fully comprehend its impact on financial performance or quality of everyday life in the workplace. No stakeholder, except for competitors, would be happy if they knew the costs added to the goods or services that they purchase due to 'fat' behaviors."

The paper showed the tremendous amount of behavioral waste that leaders normally exhibit and how it undercuts respect and other value-added behaviors, which are absolutely required to make the Lean management system work. The "Respect for People" principle is not optional.

The 2003 Shingo Prize winning book *Better Thinking, Better Results: Case Study and Analysis of an Enterprise-Wide Lean Transformation* helped answer the question: "How do you conduct a Lean transformation?" It was a detailed case study and analysis of The Wiremold Company's enterprise-wide Lean transformation from 1991-2001. It presented Lean as a management system and was the first book to describe the application and integration of the "Continuous Improvement" and "Respect for People" principles in a business not affiliated with Toyota or its key suppliers.

Finally, the "Respect for People" principle has long existed in Toyota Motor Corporation's relationship with its customers through its "customer-first" rule [1, 13]. The "Respect for People" principle also exists in Toyota's relationship with its key suppliers, where the focus since 1939 has been joint problem solving and capability-building instead of bargaining over prices, long-term relationships, and co-prosperity. The results of this policy, introduced by Kiichiro Toyoda, the first president of Toyota Motor Corporation, are truly remarkable and have been extensively documented in recent years [22-26]. In addition, investors and communities have long been treated with respect and experienced mutual prosperity. This illustrates the broader intent and meaning of the "Respect for People" principle, which should really be understood as "Respect for Stakeholders" [1].

So there you have it; a quick tour of the origins and evolution of the "Respect for People" principle, and some of the books and papers in which it has appeared over time. This principle has been a consistent theme in Toyota's management thinking and practice – and before that also in the thinking and practice of Scientific Management.

Unfortunately, not only have most senior managers been unaware of, or, ignored the "Respect for People" principles for decades, but almost the entire Lean community outside of Toyota Motor Corporation has done so as well. Ignoring or failing to apply this fundamental principle over that last 30 years has surely held back the sincere efforts of both Lean advocates and Lean practitioners.

Jim Womack's e-mail note closed with a challenge:

"The challenge for those of us in the Lean community is to embrace and explain the true nature of mutual respect for people – managers and associates…."

Womack's statement is supported by advocates of both Lean management and Scientific Management. After all, it is the "Respect for People" principle that makes Lean management work.

However, we must enlarge the challenge. We must embrace and explain how the "Respect for People" principle is a required part of the Lean management system, and that it extends beyond the narrow manager-associate dyad to encompass other people: customers, suppliers, investors, and communities. We must help senior managers understand that the "Respect for People" principle is inclusive of all key stakeholders, and how they can consistently apply the principle both day-to-day and strategically and in combination with the "Continuous Improvement" principle.

The focus of my four books and over a dozen papers written in the last decade has been to present Lean as a management system, to illuminate the "Respect for People" principle, and to describe the interplay between the "Respect for People" and "Continuous Improvement" principles [27-30].

Business leaders who want to know more about how to bring the "Respect for People" principle to life will benefit from reading the new workbook, *Practical Lean Leadership: A Strategic Leadership Guide for Executives* [31]. But remember this: words printed on paper can be very helpful but are never sufficient. The "Respect for People" and "Continuous Improvement" principles are comprehended only through daily thinking and practice on-the-job.

In closing, you will have a pretty good basic understanding of Lean management when you can articulate how the "Respect for People" principle relates to takt time, standardized work, 5

Whys, heijunka, jidoka, just-in-time, set-up reduction, kanban, poka-yoke, kaizen, and visual controls, for each of the following categories of people: employees, suppliers, customers, investors, and communities – for all of these 11 items in all five categories, not just for a couple of items in one or two categories.

The "Respect for People" principle is anything but trivial to understand.

Notes

[1] "The Toyota Way 2001," Toyota Motor Corporation, internal document, Toyota City, Japan, April 2001

[2] F.W. Taylor, *The Principles of Scientific Management*, Harper & Brothers Publishers, New York, NY, 1911

[3] W. Tsutsui, *Manufacturing Ideology: Scientific Management in Twentieth-Century Japan*, Princeton University Press, Princeton, New Jersey, 1998

[4] R. Whatley Cooke-Taylor, *Modern Factory System*, Kegan Paul, Trench, Trubner & Co., Ltd., London, 1891, pp. 459-461

[5] F.W. Taylor, "Shop Management," *Transactions of The American Society of Mechanical Engineers*, Vol. 25, 1903, pp. 1337-1480

[6] H.S. Person, "Leadership in Scientific Management" in *Scientific Management in American Industry*, The Taylor Society, Harper and Brothers Publishers, New York, NY, 1929, pp. 427-439

[7] For more on understanding the "Respect for People" principle and its literal translation from Japanese, see the blog posting "Exploring the 'Respect for People' Principle of the Toyota Way" by Jon Miller dated 4 February 2008, www.gembapantarei.com/2008/02/exploring_the_respect_for_people_principle_of_the.html. See also Y. Sugimori, K. Kusunoki, F. Cho, and S. Uchikawa, "Toyota Production System and Kanban System Materialization of Just-in-Time and Respect-for-Human System," *International Journal of Production Research*, Vol. 15, No. 6, 1977, pp. 553-564

[8] Toyota Motor Corporation, "Sustainability Report 2007," p. 57,www.toyota.co.jp/en/environmental_rep/07/download/index.html

[9] J.P. Womack, "Respect for People," e-mail to the Lean community, 20 December 2007, www.lean.org

[10] Toyota Motor Corporation, "Guiding Principles" www.toyota.co.jp/en/vision/philosophy/index.html and "Contribution Towards Sustainable Development" www.toyota.co.jp/en/vision/sustainability/index.html

[11] M.L. Emiliani, "Lean Behaviors," *Management Decision*, Vol. 36, No. 9, pp. 615-631, 1998

[12] F. W. Taylor, *Scientific Management: Comprising Shop Management, Principles of Scientific Management,Testimony Before the House Committee*, foreword by Harlow S. Person, Harper & Brothers Publishers, New York, NY, 1947

[13] S. Kamiya, *My Life With Toyota*, Toyota Motor Sales Co., Ltd., 1976, pp. 31, 48

[14] Y. Sugimori, K. Kusunoki, F. Cho, and S. Uchikawa, "Toyota Production System and Kanban System Materialization of Just-in-Time and Respect-for-Human System," *International Journal of Production Research*, Vol. 15, No. 6, 1977, pp. 553-564

[15] S. Kato, *My Years with Toyota*, Toyota Motor Sales Co., Ltd., 1981, p. 101

[16] Y. Monden, *Toyota Production System: Practical Approach to Production Management*, Industrial Engineering and Management Press, Norcross, GA, 1983, p. 11 and 141

[17] T. Ohno, *Toyota Production System: Beyond Large-Scale Production*, Productivity Press, Portland, OR, 1988, p. xiii

[18] M. Imai, *Kaizen: The Key to Japan's Competitive Success*, McGraw-Hill, New York, NY, 1987

[19] M. Imai, "Introduction to Kaizen," Kaizen Institute of America seminar at The Hartford Graduate Center, Hartford, Conn., May 9, 1988

[20] M. Husar, "Corporate Culture: Toyota's Secret, Competitive Advantage," General Motors internal paper, 16 May 1991, pp. 10-11

[21]. Y. Togo, *Yuki Togo's Sell Like Hell!!*, self-published, 1997, pp. 141-142

[22] J. Womack, D. Jones, and D. Roos, *The Machine that Changed the World*, Rawson Associates, New York, NY, 1990, Chapter 6
[23] T. Nishiguchi, *Strategic Industrial Sourcing*, Oxford University Press, New York, NY, 1994
[24] T. Fujimoto, *The Evolution of a Manufacturing System at Toyota*, Oxford University Press, Inc., New York, NY, 1999
[25] J. Dyer and K. Nobeoka, "Creating and Managing a High Performance Knowledge-Sharing Network: The Toyota Case," *Strategic Management Journal*, Vol. 21, No. 3, 2000, pp. 345-367
[26] J. Liker and T. Choi, "Building Deep Supplier Relationships," *Harvard Business Review*, December 2004, pp. 104-113
[27] B. Emiliani, with D. Stec, L. Grasso, and J. Stodder, *Better Thinking, Better Results: Case Study and Analysis of an Enterprise-Wide Lean Transformation*, second edition, The CLBM, LLC, Wethersfield, Conn., 2007
[28] B. Emiliani, *REAL LEAN: Understanding the Lean Management System*, Volume One, The CLBM, LLC, Wethersfield, Conn., 2007
[29] B. Emiliani, *REAL LEAN: Critical Issues and Opportunities in Lean Management*, Volume Two, The CLBM, LLC, Wethersfield, Conn., 2007
[30] For a list of key papers, see www.bobemiliani.com/wp-content/uploads/2013/03/list_of_papers.pdf
[31] B. Emiliani, *Practical Lean Leadership: A Strategic Leadership Guide for Executives*, The CLBM, LLC, Wethersfield, Conn., 2008

Lesson 2

Do Your Homework

A good way to start Lean management in organizations is for senior managers to first do a bit of homework. Specifically, senior managers should be aware of the common complaints and criticisms about Lean that they can expect to receive from key stakeholders, particularly employees.

The criticisms from employees today are nearly the same as they were over 100 years ago when modern progressive management was first introduced into organizations. They are:

- De-humanize them
- Speed them up and burn them out
- De-skill them
- Take away their knowledge
- Take away their creativity
- Cost them their job

Understanding employees' perspectives and effectively responding to their concerns and criticisms will go a long way towards making your Lean transformation a success.

Executives who have a better understanding of the intent and purpose of Lean management will be better equipped to alleviate employee's fears and gain buy-in for Lean throughout the enterprise.

Unfortunately, most Lean transformations do not begin with a clear understanding of employees concerns, the root causes of those concerns, and the application of practical countermeasures. As a result, many organizations find they have to do quite a bit of re-work later on.

If ever there was re-work worth doing, however, it is for executives to go back and understand the perspectives of employees, and for the entire management team to formulate a consistent and effective response that generates great enthusiasm for the daily application of non-zero-sum (win-win) continuous improvement.

Doing so would be one way of putting the "Respect for People" principle into action.

Lesson 3

Start with REAL Lean

Does an organization need to start with Fake Lean? Is that a key part of the learning process on the way to REAL Lean?

Given the pervasiveness of Fake Lean, one would think it is a necessary step along the way. However, it is necessary only if senior managers are misinformed about Lean management by people who, at the start, do not know Lean well or who intentionally guide management towards Fake Lean.

Most senior managers mistakenly assume that Lean is something to bolt-on to their existing understanding and practice of management. They do not realize in the beginning that Lean management replaces most of their existing understanding and practice of management. They learn this years after they started, if at all.

Fake Lean, therefore, does not have to be part of the learning process to get to REAL Lean. In fact, most that start out with Fake Lean usually remain stuck on Fake Lean by choice or by ignorance. Some think Fake Lean is good enough, while others think Fake Lean is the same as REAL Lean. Fake Lean can appear to be a part of the learning process on the way to REAL Lean when senior managers do not learn and evolve in their thinking and practice of Lean.

So the answer to the questions, "Does an organization need to start with Fake Lean? Is that a key part of the learning process on the way to REAL Lean?", is "No." Organizations do not have to start with Fake Lean. Why? Because today, unlike decades ago, many resources are available to help senior managers understand the difference between Fake Lean and REAL Lean management before they begin their Lean transformation.

There is no doubt that a phenomenon has long existed which I call "Lean confusion," meaning, managers have difficulty understanding the difference between Fake Lean to REAL Lean, and the path from one to the other remains unclear. Many resources have become available in recent years specifically reduce "Lean confusion" and avoid getting stuck on Fake Lean.

Executives must establish REAL Lean as the target condition to strive for, and create standardized work for themselves and others to steadily move towards the target condition.

Lesson 4

Off To a Bad Start with Lean Tools

Lean tools are often seen as the gateway to inspire people to become more interested in Lean management and dig deeper into its meaning and intent. That is indeed true for some people who use the tools as part of their organization's operating system. But, it usually is not true for senior managers because few actually practice the Lean tools that they tell others to practice.

While obviously necessary and very helpful, the tools used correctly help people learn and improve processes in remarkable ways. However, the danger, as we have long known, is that Lean tools become both the beginning and end of Lean for many people. Lean tools are misunderstood as Lean management itself, devoid of the changes in beliefs, behaviors, and competencies that must occur, particularly among senior managers. As expected, managers are satisfied when workers use Lean tools because they get exactly what they want: quick cost savings, etc., with no effort on their part.

The premise that the use of Lean tools leads to greater interest in Lean management has led to vast amounts of tool-based training over the last four decades. Yet, there are few organizations that practice Lean management with distinction; meaning, both the "Continuous Improvement" and "Respect for People" principles. Thus, the premise is faulty as a generalization and spawns a completely inaccurate characterization of Lean tools training as "Lean leadership."

Overwhelming empirical evidence tells us that starting senior managers off with Lean tools training is a big mistake. Why? Because it does not inform them of the specific, practical differences between conventional management and Lean management across four critical dimensions: economic, social, political, and historical. Ignoring these dimensions means that Lean management will not advance far in any organization or industry.

It is clear to me that Lean transformations are paced by the willingness of leaders to question their economic, social, political, and historical beliefs about business, management, and leadership. These are the major barriers, and therefore a much better place to start Lean management training. In addition, it will establish for executives the foundation for their practice of Lean tools.

You can learn more about this in *Moving Forward Faster*, which describes 85 economic, social, and political ideas that must diminish or be eliminated, and historical facts that must be understood and acknowledged in order to experience long-term success with Lean management.

It is a provocative little book that will challenge and enliven you. At about 100 pages, it is a quick read and also a very important read. I am sure that you find it helpful.

Lesson 5

Do Not Forget the "Respect for People" Principle

Most thought leaders in the Lean community attribute the cause of Lean failure to a focus on Lean tools themselves instead of using the tools for daily practice of improvement and coaching katas. Their perspective is that practicing a new *behavior* pattern, called an "improvement kata," leads to a new *belief*. This may be true in the specific case of a power-based relationship, such as supervisor-subordinate, but I have long seen it the other way around - particularly for senior managers. New beliefs lead to new behaviors, which, in turn, result in new competencies.

In order for Lean management to succeed, there must first be in place a belief among people, particularly associates, that applying PDCA and practicing other Lean tools is broadly beneficial. Often, this is trumped by empirical evidence where people see or directly experience zero-sum (win-lose) outcomes, such as the newspaper headline, "Philips 'Best Plant' Slated to Close in Sparta," or the company's profits increase but associates do not receive higher wages and must pay more for health insurance. These zero-sum outcomes are powerful deterrents to practicing Lean tools or improvement katas. People will not respond to challenges where they are certain to be the loser. Lean management is obviously on the path to failure when that happens.

We know that for Lean to succeed, it must be practiced in non-zero-sum (win-win) ways. That is why the "Respect for People" principle, or something very similar to it, has been around since the beginning of modern progressive management over 100 years ago. Toyota has done a pretty good job with this, which greatly facilitates practicing improvement katas. Most other organizations have not.

Let me use an analogy to explain why beliefs precede behaviors. Suppose someone wants to learn how to play the guitar. The prospective musician likes the idea of being a musician, but they immediately confront some challenges: sore fingertips, confusion, and frustration, to name a few. In other words, the guitar wins and the player loses, typically for quite some time. The punishment for the beginner exists in the present and is large, while the rewards are unknown and far into the future. Not surprisingly, most people who try to play music quit after a short time. Reality trumps their idea of wanting to be a musician, unless there is a power-based relationship: i.e. parent-child or teacher-student.

If, instead, the prospective musician possesses a belief at the start that learning to play the guitar will be beneficial, then they possess the fundamental belief that drives the behavior to practice playing the guitar every day for years. They will persevere in response to the challenge and transcend the zero-sum outcomes they experienced as beginners. The player starts winning, without necessarily needing a power-based relationship to direct purposeful daily practice. The belief leads to new behaviors, which results in new competencies: being a capable musician. They will continue to practice daily because it is fun and rewarding.

Economies of scale provides another example of why beliefs must precede behaviors. Nearly every senior manager unconditionally accepts economies of scale; that production costs decline as volumes increase. What, then, is the new behavior that must be practiced for them to reject economies of scale, which breaks down as flow improves? Behavior change will not occur if senior managers believe, with absolutely certainty, that production costs decline as volumes increase. They have to believe it is beneficial to question their fundamental understanding of economics. Most just won't do it; they have no interest in changing their basic way of thinking.

Disciplined use of improvement and coaching katas will help people move toward their future state - provided they believe that doing so will not result in zero-sum outcomes. That is management's challenge; it is their responsibility to prove it. They have to accept and apply, every day, in ways large and small, the "Respect for People" principle and consistently demonstrate non-zero-sum outcomes to associates and other key stakeholders. If not, Lean will fail.

Lesson 6

Fake Lean vs. Fun Lean

Sometime in late 2000 or early 2001, I coined the phrase "Fake Lean." I had also been using the term "Imitation Lean," but decided that "Fake Lean" was a better expression to describe the tool-based focus on continuous improvement that had become ubiquitous. I felt there needed to be a simple phrase to distinguish between the many who focused only on continuous improvement, usually in a zero-sum (win-lose) way, compared to the few who practiced both principles of Lean management, "Continuous Improvement" and "Respect for People" in a non-zero-sum (win-win) way.

Then in 2003, in the book *Better Thinking, Better Results*, I described a distinction between "scary style" kaizen and "human style" kaizen (page 66, note 15). I wish I would have thought more about that. I now realize it might have been far better to characterize the two ways of understanding and practicing Lean management as "Scary Lean" and "Fun Lean."

Scary Lean is where workers are forced to participate in kaizen, after which some get laid off, thus making kaizen an extremely undesirable experience. One can only guess at the number of workers who have experienced this corrupted form of Lean, but it must be in the millions.

Imagine mom or dad going home at 11 am after getting laid off and bitterly complaining over dinner about how kaizen cost them their job. Imagine, further, the psychological distress caused by cash flow going to zero overnight and the struggle to find new employment. What must the children, little Billy or little Chandra, think of what happened to mom or dad. What will the kids think of kaizen, which has caused so much family pain? Will they embrace kaizen and Lean as workers or as managers in their future career? It does not seem likely.

Management's desire for short-term gains at the expense of other people has surely had a large negative impact on Lean management. The broad-based association of Lean with layoffs has certainly limited its impact in manufacturing. And it has also prevented Lean management from entering industries that desperately need to understand and improve their processes such as higher education (both administration and academics), or from spreading more rapidly into industries such as healthcare.

I learned "Fun Lean" from some amazing and wonderful kaizen consultants and from a former boss at the factory where I worked in the mid-1990s. Our approach to kaizen was one of experimenting, learning, improving, and having fun. We were proud of our accomplishments. And, because we had a good time, we wanted to experience kaizen again and again.

People like to be involved with things that are fun. If kaizen is made fun by management and kaizen facilitators, then people will be drawn to it. They will willingly participate in kaizen because it helps customers, is a great team experience, and is personally rewarding.

I feel fortunate to have learned "Fun Lean" but very distressed to know that so many others have known only "Scary Lean." Therefore, we must all place extraordinary emphasis on the "Respect for People" principle now and far into the future if we hope for Lean to be understood and practiced correctly by the next generation of managers and workers.

Simply focusing on more skilled application of Lean tools will be of little help if workers and others continue to experience zero-sum outcomes.

Lesson 7

History of Progressive Lean Management

Poor Frederick Winslow Taylor (1856-1915). His Scientific Management system (Lean management's antecedent) was so badly misinterpreted that he got all the blame when managers unknown, in companies large and small, misunderstood and misapplied and his principles and practices over 100 years ago. His work was so fouled-up by management practitioners and management consultants that it earned Taylor the opportunity to testify before Congress for three days in January 1912.

Taylor made good use of his time in front of Congressional investigators. The testimony he gave was the clearest articulation of his intentions and the outcomes that one can expect if Scientific Management was correctly understood and practiced by managers. In the face of intense criticism from Congressmen, Taylor succinctly summed up his position:

> "It ceases to be scientific management
> the moment it is used for bad."

All Taylor was trying to do was to improve workplace productivity without burning people out and improve cooperation between management and workers, both in a non-zero-sum (win-win) way.

It is never too late to gain a proper understanding of Taylor's work from the early 1900s because it will help you better understand Lean management in the early 2000s. I recommend reading short paper titled: "The Spirit and Social Significance of Scientific Management" [1]. It is a wonderful description of Scientific Management written by Morris Cooke, a close colleague of Frederick W. Taylor.

Cooke makes clear the importance of the worker and how they must be respected. It should be read by all serious Lean practitioners, and especially by anyone who thinks that Taylor and his colleagues had as their intent to turn workers into unthinking robots or resources to exploit.

Like Scientific Management before it, today we often find Lean turned into a mean-spirited, zero-sum corporate "initiative" to maximize efficiencies at workers' expense. The parallels between Scientific Management of the early 1900s and modern-day Fake Lean management are stunning. How unfortunate it is that so much time has passed with so little having been learned.

Most managers do not care about management history because they think things are different today. I can assure you that understanding the history of progressive management will help you do a better job of practicing REAL Lean management today and in the future.

My *REAL LEAN* books, Volumes Two and Three, contain extensive accounts of the early history of progressive management. You will be amazed by what you read.

Notes

[1] "The Spirit and Social Significance of Scientific Management," M. L. Cooke, *Journal of Political Economy*, Vol. 21, No. 6 (June, 1913), pp. 481-493, www.jstor.org/stable/1819267

Lesson 8

Happy Anniversary: The Toyota Way 2001

April 2011 was the tenth anniversary of the publication of Toyota Motor Corporation's internal document, "The Toyota Way 2001." I was very excited when I first heard about it because of my experience with Lean when I worked in industry, and later as a professor teaching and researching Lean management beginning in 1999. While the document was not available to people outside of Toyota, the high-level characterization that was publicly available made explicit the two principles of progressive Lean management: "Continuous Improvement" and "Respect for People."

"The Toyota Way 2001" document highlighted the importance of the "Respect for People" principle and provided an extensive description of it in four pages (the "Continuous Improvement" principle was described in six pages). The "Respect for People" principle, while new to most people, has actually been a major element of progressive management for over 100 years (see Lesson 1: "The Equally Important 'Respect for People' Principle"). This makes sense because for a management system to be progressive, it must obviously be substantially different and more advanced than current alternatives.

It is impossible to overstate the importance of the "Respect for People" principle because that is what truly distinguishes Lean management from conventional management. Without managers' consistent daily application of this principle, the best they can hope to achieve is discontinuous improvement, and backslide is assured. Without it, executives will remain stuck with their mostly conventional zero-sum (win-lose) management practice. With the "Respect for People" principle, they can create a far more desirable non-zero-sum (win-win) management system in which daily continuous improvement thrives. This will have far greater appeal to all key business stakeholders: employees, suppliers, customers, investors, and communities.

Amazingly, Toyota Way 2001 went largely unrecognized by the Lean community for almost seven years due to the enduring focus on Lean tools - an era lasting over 30 years and dubbed "The Tool Age." While we have finally begun to move out of the tool age, the "Respect for People" principle today remains barely recognized and its significance is poorly understood. Most people remain committed to "The Toyota Half-Way," meaning, recognizing and practicing only the "Continuous Improvement" principle - what I have long called "Fake Lean."

Most managers do not understand what the "Respect for People" principle means and they struggle to put it into daily practice - assuming they have even heard of it. Nor do they understand that "people" must include employees, suppliers, customers, investors, and communities. As a result, they cannot comprehend the decisive role the "Respect for People" principle plays in all successful Lean transformations.

One critical aspect of Lean which people do not even think about is the very important yet subtle relationship between the "Continuous Improvement" and "Respect for People" principles. A lack of awareness of this relationship has led to widespread cherry-picking of Lean tools and the expansion of Fake Lean.

If your Lean transformation is tool-based or limited in scope to operations, then you would be wise to lean the unique leadership beliefs, behaviors, and competencies needed to make that happen.

Lesson 9

Leaders and Information Flow

Leadership is defined in so many different ways - and usually only from the perspective of the leader, not the followers - that it is extremely difficult to clearly understand what constitutes good leadership. That, coupled with media coverage of C-level business executives hailed as great leaders, when in fact many are extremely poor leaders (highly-paid zero-sum cost cutters), only adds to the confusion. A simpler and more effective way to think about leadership, and, in particular, Lean leadership, is to focus on these two hallmarks of excellent leadership:

- Beliefs, behaviors, and competencies that facilitate material and information flow.
- Having an acute sense of time, where time is understood to be a treasure that cannot be wasted.

Academics who study leadership do not make the connection between leadership, material and information flow, and time. They have no reason to because, to them, leadership is seen as something separate. They focus narrowly on specific behaviors or personal characteristics such as charisma, and do not recognize material and information flow and time as characteristics – indeed, the basic function – of great leadership. I do, and so should you. Call it "flow leadership."

Flow leaders let people think, improve, create, and innovate. People know about problems and opportunities sooner, have greater awareness of changes going on around them, and are responsive to change. They hear the voice of the customer more clearly, and that of all stakeholders. And, the leadership team communicates better among themselves and with others. Organizational politics is reduced to very low levels so as not to obscure reality and degrade logical thinking and decision-making.

Being a follower under a flow leader is a lot more fun and a much better learning experience from both technical and managerial perspectives. Flow leaders are excellent role models. An organization with flow leaders at the top organically creates great leaders from which to draw upon in the future.

If you think back to the best bosses you have ever had, you will recognize them as being skilled in facilitating material and information flow, and of having a good sense of time - though they may have known nothing at all about Lean management. What they did understand was how their behaviors affected other people and their ability to quickly process material and information.

Innovative organizations are often led by flow leaders. Their leadership helps deliver a steady stream of innovations that have positive human and economic impact. Organizations need people in every department to innovate every day, not just periodically when they need to get out of a hole they dug for themselves. The connection between flow leadership and innovation is under-appreciated, if not completely overlooked.

Organizations that can consistently innovate enjoy so many benefits (as do their stakeholders) that flow leadership should be highly sought after by every senior manager and required by every board of directors.

Lesson 10

Faulty Thinking and Decision-Making

Are you aware of how common bad leadership is? Perhaps you have a general sense of it, but my decade-plus polling of a few thousand undergraduate and graduate students with full or part-time jobs reveals that about 90% of those in management positions range from mediocre to awful leaders. It seems that the great majority of people in leadership positions do not act like leaders of people. Instead, their most important duties apparently are meetings, metrics, and their boss, not the people that they serve. Into this netherworld they go, developing and refining the two hallmarks of bad leadership:

- Beliefs, behaviors, and competencies that obstruct material and information flow.
- Having an indiscriminate sense of time, meaning, time is plentiful and can be freely wasted.

Bad leaders cause widespread delays and rework by batching material and information. They restrict and withhold information, giving only what they deem to be important, and are quick to blame people for errors. These disrespectful behaviors are faithfully returned to management by workers who are afraid to speak up when they discover abnormal conditions.

While most bosses hate surprises, the persistence of blocked information flows means they better get used to them. Such organizations struggle to create innovative products and services or experience an uneven run of hits and misses. Can a major product line or business failure be far away?

For several years I have taught a unique graduate course that I created in which we formally analyze major business failure using A4 reports (similar to A3 reports). We use it to analyze and document the failures, including the identification of senior managers' untested beliefs and assumptions, decision-making traps, illogical thinking, say-do gaps, etc. These elements of human behavior greatly enlarge student's understanding of a management problem and its causes.

Despite the wide range of companies, industries, products and services, and people involved, students are always amazed at the broad, and often specific, similarities between the different failures. They learn that the common view among senior managers, that they or their situation is different, is deeply flawed. And, with each failure there are always massive problems with information flow. Management loses its sense of time and problems are unknown, or purposefully avoided. Problems linger unaddressed for years, if not for decades.

Your situation is not so different, but thinking that it is means you will not learn from the mistakes of others. This puts you and the organization at greater risk. The multi-million and multi-billion dollar mistakes made by others are a cornucopia of free consulting if you are willing to study them. Along the way, you must carefully examine your own untested beliefs and assumptions, faulty logic, and propensity to fall into common decisions-making traps.

Managers are often very quick to point out to others that they cannot improve if they do not know about problems. But, when it comes to management thinking and decision-making, most are unaware of or ignore this as a major source of problems. That is too bad, because faulty management thinking and decision-making are perhaps the most significant source of problems.

You can learn how we analyze business failures in my book, *Moving Forward Faster* (Appendix IV). A small $30 investment can easily pay you back one million-fold or more.

Lesson 11

Antidote for Dysfunction

In the previous Lesson, I mentioned that for several years I have taught a unique graduate course that I created in which we formally analyze major business failures. The results that we see are consistent from case-to-case, irrespective of product made, service offered, or industry. That is, people in high positions think that simply being in a high position assures rigorous thinking and accurate decision-making. In other words, their ability to process information is assumed to be sound.

Instead, we find the opposite: Leaders are mistake-prone due to faulty assumptions, the ease with which they fall into decision-making traps, and the pervasive use of illogical thinking. High position greatly reduces the likelihood of rigorous thinking and accurate decision-making, and instead increases the probability that big mistakes will be made. The case for lowering one's ego and becoming more humble and open-minded could not be greater because bad decisions negatively impact the lives of stakeholders, often in substantial ways.

So, what's a leader to do? Leaders mired in conventional management will not really care about faulty assumptions, decision-making traps, and illogical thinking because that is what everyone does in conventional management. This is closely tied to the political routines commonly found in organizations. In addition, it is common for executive decision-making processes to lack standards, which leads to variability, errors, and higher costs.

Lean management offers a ready and very effective antidote for this problem: kaizen. Done right, kaizen quickly exposes faulty assumptions, eliminates decision-making traps, and corrects illogical thinking. It requires people to see and understand things as they actually are, with nothing standing in the way to obscure reality.

The problem is, of course, most senior managers do not participate in kaizen. If they did, they would come away from those experiences with a better capacity to think clearly and make better decisions. The typical outcome is less organizational politics because kaizen changes the conversation. What organization would not benefit from less politics?

Organizational politics creates no value for end-use customers and offers no benefits to any stakeholder. It is nothing more than waste, unevenness, and unreasonableness in human interaction. In addition to creating waste, unevenness, and unreasonableness in human interactions (processes), organizational politics contributes greatly to the existence waste, unevenness, and unreasonableness in physical processes.

There is a deeper connection to be made here. Organizational politics *requires* faulty assumptions, decision-making traps, and illogical thinking. Think of it the other way around; few people would recognize politics as being the citadel of sound assumptions, good decisions, and logical thinking. Far from it. Organizational politics increase costs and voraciously consumes resources, especially time, which can never be recovered.

Think about this: The faulty assumptions, decision-making traps, and illogical thinking that develops in executives over time due to organizational politics becomes the dominant routine for thinking about business and related decision-making. Is it any wonder why we see so much corporate distress, not to mention the human suffering that always accompanies bad thinking and flawed decisions? Organizational politics destroys good business thinking and severely degrades decision-making.

So why, you ask, don't more companies visibly suffer from the consequences of organizational politics? In most cases, it is because they can afford to pay for all the mistakes and delays.

You have to fail badly to have it result in a takeover or bankruptcy. Needless to say, paying for mistakes big and small is a bad use of money. But until stakeholders demand improved thinking from executives, it is a corporate expense - a large tax - that they and other stakeholders must pay, and pay in increasing amounts as organizational politics becomes more dominant.

Organizational politics is completely man made and can therefore be reduced or eliminated. That is one of the great lessons learned in my book *Better Thinking, Better Results.* Lean management and, more specifically, kaizen, can help eliminate people's dependence on organizational politics as the principal mechanism for normalizing chaos (as I described in Chapter 7 of *REAL LEAN*, Volume 6, "Crazy Processes, Krazy Managers").

Lesson 12

Kaizen, Not Kaizen Event

One of the tragedies of Lean management is the phrase "kaizen event," and related phrases such as "kaizen blitz" or "kaizen project." The proper usage is simply "kaizen," without the word "event," "blitz," "project," or any other word attached to it.

The word "event" likely was attached to "kaizen" in 1987, when Shingijutsu Co. Ltd. conducted their first kaizens at Jacobs Vehicle Equipment Company in Bloomfield, Connecticut. To people experiencing kaizen for the first time, it probably did seem like an "event." But this is actually an aberration as kaizen is a daily activity. The week-long, event-like format was established for the convenience of the Shingijutsu kaizen consultants traveling from Japan.

The phrase "kaizen event" has had the unfortunate, widespread impact of promoting sporadic kaizen, and of managers counting the number of kaizens as evidence of continuous improvement. In reality, they are counting dis-continuous improvement. Further, the corporatization of continuous improvement means that a centralized office determines the best way to do kaizens and the hurdles people must surmount to become "certified" Lean leaders. Placing extensive structure on top of simple kaizen means that people will take kaizen less seriously, avoid participating in kaizen, or game the kaizen metric to check the box. The result: all the fun is taken out of kaizen.

Kaizen done right should be a lot of fun for everyone involved - a lot of fun. Often, when people are trained in kaizen, the three principles of kaizen are never mentioned. They are:

- Process and results
- Systems focus
- Non-blaming, non-judgmental.

When these principles are left out of kaizen training, or ignored by management, people suffer. They often lose employment as a result of kaizen, and that's no fun. Unthinking leaders have transformed kaizen from an opportunity for everyone to learn and improve, to a great threat and something to avoid.

I prefer to remain faithful to original phrases and their original meanings. I always recommend to people that they simply refer to kaizen as "kaizen" - which literally means "change for the better," from a multi-lateral perspective. Kaizen must never result in an improvement in one work area while causing problems in another upstream or downstream work area, nor should an internal improvement cause problems for any external stakeholder such as suppliers or customers.

Changing "kaizen" to some other name, such as "rapid improvement workshop" loses connectivity to the fact that kaizen must be practiced in a non-zero-sum (win-win) way. Once the word "kaizen" disappears, so does its three principles: process and results; systems view; and non-blaming, non-judgmental. Therefore, improvement immediately degrades into zero-sum, ROI-driven, results-focused "events" to improve narrow work activities isolated from the bigger picture, coupled with management that likely continues to blame people for errors and judge them for past problems.

Kaizen is actually quite difficult to understand beyond its common surface-level meaning of "continuous improvement." Small errors in management's understanding of kaizen invariably lead to big problems which can quickly result in perfunctory improvement activities, and, eventually, the death of continuous improvement in organizations. Therefore, it is essential for senior managers to participate in kaizen. It is the only way for them to learn the details and nuances of kaizen that are necessary for its continuing practice.

To help you get started, please read *Kaizen Forever: Teachings of Chihiro Nakao.*

Lesson 13

Bad Practice Theory

Every now and then an article appears in an influential publication that briefly takes the wind out of your sails. One such article recently appeared in *The Wall Street Journal* titled: "For Lean Factories, No Buffer." The typical problem that one encounters is that the writer has little or no knowledge of Lean and therefore misunderstands and misrepresents it. That is indeed true of this article. More important, however, is what the executives and others interviewed in the article have to say about Just-in-Time – which is mistakenly presented as synonymous with Lean.

Why does it take the wind out of your sails? Because despite 30 or more years of work by many people to explain and teach JIT, the top executives cited in the article still do not understand it. Nor do the purchasing executive, consultants, or economist cited in the article. Teachers hate it when students do not learn. They hate it even more when former students do not bother to engage in research and self-study of topics that are of great importance to their work and careers.

In the article, the CEO of Terex says:

> "Just-in-time makes sense, but it's vulnerable to disruptions."

True enough, and so is batch-and-queue processing. In fact, batch-and-queue generates many more disruptions than JIT, but it does not seem that way to executives because people deep in the organization labor furiously to do work-arounds. As a result, the true nature of problems go uncorrected and will be repeated. In contrast, JIT (done right, along with the other components of the management system - autonomation, heijunka, standardized work, visual controls, etc.) demands that problems be understood and practical countermeasures must be applied to avoid repeat errors.

The Terex CEO goes on to say:

> "...so what we are seeing is the theoretical being adapted to meet the world of the practical."

JIT is not theoretical. JIT done wrong does not make JIT theoretical; it is simply JIT done wrong. What the Terex CEO saw in his company was JIT done wrong from a technical perspective, and also from a behavioral perspective (zero-sum, win-lose, JIT). Characterizing JIT as "theory" is simply an excuse for having done a bad job, and for not wanting to admit it or take responsibility.

It would be more accurate for the Terex CEO to have said:

> "...so what we are seeing is our faulty version of JIT being adapted to create bigger safety buffers because we don't actually understand JIT and probably never will."

This is nothing more than moving backwards, with the CEO leading the efforts to un-improve. That explains the $1.7 billion of inventory on $4.1 billion in COGS (2.4 inventory turns).

Instead, what the Terex CEO should have done long ago and have been able to say today is:

> "Just-in-time still makes sense. We are working daily to improve JIT and supporting practices by identifying the actual root causes of problems in a non-blaming way and engaging in joint problem-solving with our suppliers. By working very closely with our suppliers, mutually beneficial outcomes are achieved that include lower costs, higher quality, and better on-time delivery performance. Performance is improving across all of our supply

> chains. We benefit just as much as our suppliers benefit, and no longer does one party improve at another's expense. Our suppliers are much happier; go see for yourself."

The article claims that JIT "theory is stumbling in practice." That characterization is completely backwards; it is bad practice theory that is stumbling in JIT.

Look no further than the erroneous practice theory offered by the strategic sourcing executive: "In a just-in-time environment, you let suppliers figure out what you'll need six or seven months out."

And the teacher screams, "Arrggghhh!!"

Lesson 14

Improving Gemba Walks

For decades, the focus of gemba walks by visitors has been on operations. Specifically, to observe the value-creating work, evaluate processes, and look for evidence of continuous improvement using Lean methods and tools. While certainly beneficial, doing this has never been sufficient. Gemba walks must expand beyond operations and, more importantly, have a strong focus on the "Respect for People" principle. This improvement in gemba walks is long overdue.

A gemba walk whose focus is better balanced on both Lean principles, "Continuous Improvement" and "Respect for People," will help visitors learn if the company's Lean efforts are REAL or Fake. In addition, this will challenge senior managers to understand and practice the "Respect for People" principle and set an example for others to follow.

The "Respect for People" principle in the context of gemba walks must, of course, include all key stakeholders: employees, suppliers, customers, investors, and communities. Evidence for the "Respect for People" principle must be evaluated in combination with observation of processes and the proper application of continuous improvement tools. The "Continuous Improvement" principle is well-defined and can be objectively evaluated. Can the same be said for the "Respect for People" principle? Yes it can. Here are some examples:

1) Zero-sum management decisions and outcomes (win-lose) are simple, yet very revealing indicators of the absence of the "Respect for People" principle. If there is no qualified job guarantee - no layoffs due to kaizen - the "Respect for People" principle is absent. If there is no quarterly profit sharing (e.g. 15% of pre-tax income divided by total straight time wages), then the "Respect for People" principle is absent. If there is

huge pay disparity between workers and the president/CEO, then the "Respect for People" principle is absent. We cannot forget that real wages of workers in the U.S. have declined by more than 10% over the last 35 years.

2) Management usually emphasizes physical safety, but what about mental safety? Is there fear in the workplace? Are people afraid of managers? Are people blamed for making errors? Management should have a no-blame policy and there should be clear evidence of its practice. Are workers being put in harm's way by working to metrics that are designed for batch-and-queue: for example, purchase price variance and earned hours? Are employees being set-up to fail?

3) How does the senior management team process information? Is it batch or flow? It should obviously be flow, and one should look for clear evidence of this. If wasteful, zero-sum organizational politics thrives, then it is 100 percent certain that information is processed batch-and-queue. Is information shared or is it closely guarded? Is there profit sharing? This is another form of information sharing; it says to people, "We did well," or, "We need to improve."

4) Is there mutual respect between the various functions and disciplines? Too often, there are wasteful rivalries between departments (e.g. engineering and operations, finance and manufacturing, etc.). Is there mutual respect for stakeholders: employees, suppliers, customers, investors, and communities? Senior managers often say "customer-first," but their decisions and actions are actually "shareholder-first." That indicates a lack of balance.

5) Lean managers focus on developing employees, but do they develop other stakeholders as well? Do they develop suppliers (including minority and women-owned businesses), do they improve investors' understanding of Lean management, etc. What has management done to improve relations with suppliers? Or are they squeezing them on price using reverse auctions? Are

senior managers personally involved in kaizen to develop their own problem-solving capabilities and then applying what they learned to their job? If not, then they are not developing themselves and not leading by example.

6) Do executives recognize inter-connections between the different functional areas? Are they siloed in their responsibilities or cross-functional? Does human resources accept any responsibility for the performance of operations; finance for quality; engineering for on-time delivery, etc.? If not, then responsibility is not being taken by senior managers. If zero-sum organizational politics thrives, then, once again, responsibility is not being taken by senior managers.

Shop and office gemba walks should have evolved long ago to include the "Respect for People" principle because this principle is the major shortcoming of nearly all Lean transformations. There is no way that Lean management can be sustained without the "Respect for People" principle, and there is no way that gemba walks focused only on the "Continuous Improvement" principle can assure sustainability. So, please improve your gemba walk, as a visitor or as a manager, as this can only help establish and perpetuate REAL Lean and help put Fake Lean in our rear-view mirror.

Lesson 15

The Importance of Daily Practice

"Practice makes perfect." You have heard that phrase a million times. While practice may not actually make "perfect," practice will surely make very good if not great. To excel in sports, music, dance, etc., one must practice a lot, every day, not once or twice a month. It will take about 10,000 hours of practice to gain proficiency, which is merely the starting point for more advanced practice. Unfortunately, practice is seen by most people as boring, so they never become skilled in the activity. To them, the pain of practice is not worth the pleasure of proficiency.

The need for purposeful daily practice in music, for example, is obvious if one wishes to be a capable musician. What is not so obvious is the need for daily practice of Lean management. Everyone in the organization, CEO on down, must practice Lean in some purposeful way every day. However, Lean has a big weakness: an executive can read 50 pages of a book on Lean, "get the idea," and support it. Lean is for everyone else to do, but the executive supports it. Unfortunately, executives cannot possibly understand Lean without many years of daily practice.

Let's say I want to make a coffee table out of wood, and that I approach this in the same way that many executives approach Lean. I read part of a book on woodworking and comprehend that making a coffee table involves cutting wood, planing, joining, drilling, nailing, screwing, gluing, sanding, finishing. OK, yeah, I got the idea. I'm done. I don't need to actually make a coffee table to know how one is made; I have sufficient book knowledge and can delegate the task of making a coffee table to other people. That is what most executives do with Lean management; they get the idea and then delegate the doing to others.

You cannot possibly know how to make a coffee table without actually doing the work, many times. You will learn, through book study, trial-and-error, and perhaps coaching as well, that mis-measuring wastes wood, it's easy to plane wood too thin, join the wrong surface, drill holes in the wrong places, use the wrong nails or screws, use too much glue, or get a lousy finish. All good carpenters have at least the tip of one finger missing. They learned their trade the hard way: through lots of practice and even some pain.

You cannot possibly know Lean management without actually practicing Lean every day. You will learn, through book study, trial-and-error, and likely coaching as well, that it is easy to misunderstand and misapply Lean principles and practices. All good Lean leaders have at least the tip of their ego missing. They too learned their trade the hard way: through lots of practice and even some pain.

I have emphasized the importance of purposeful practice since I first started writing about Lean leadership in 1998 and teaching Lean in 1999. A few years ago I created a detailed comparison between Lean and music (I play bass guitar) to emphasize the importance of daily practice and to illustrate the sonic difference between batch-and-queue and flow. It is an original and extremely creative presentation which helps senior managers better understand what they must commit to and also do in order to get the organizational learning that delivers the performance they seek. The basic message is simple: Without daily practice, you'll never understand Lean management, let alone get better at it.

The challenge in advancing Lean, and for Lean training and development for senior managers, is that most people in high-level jobs see no reason to practice something new. It is like asking someone, late in their career, who knows how to play the trumpet, to now learn how to play the drums. They are completely different instruments that require different physical coordination and mental processes (going from a treble clef instrument to bass and treble clef instrument, among other things).

Getting executives to accept deliberate, daily practice, when they simply do not want to practice something new, is a vexing problem. I call it "the music teacher's problem." A music teacher has almost nothing to teach if the student does not practice every day. I know the feeling of having many students who do not want to practice. But, every now and then I get one who does, thankfully.

Lesson 16

Bunga-Bunga Management

For many years, I have heard senior managers say that something or other is "theory" when, in fact, it is entirely practical. Remarkably, they characterize as theory things they are not familiar with; things that appear to be abstract or difficult to comprehend; things they do not know how to do; or things that seem at first glance to be unrealistic. These responses are, of course, a misunderstanding of the what word "theory" means. Something they are not familiar with is not theory; it is simply something they are not familiar with. It is not theory simply because it appears abstract, difficult to comprehend, unrealistic, or do not know how to do.

The practical consequences of this confusion can be disastrous. Thinking of something practical as theory means executives will tend to keep doing only that which they are familiar with and avoid doing anything unfamiliar (such as Lean). It compels executives to be status quo oriented, despite their endless exhortations for change, and prevents them from undertaking activities to improve customer satisfaction that are critical to the long-term success and survival of the organization.

What managers judge to be theory and what they judge to be practical is, in many cases, reversed. What they think is theory is actually practical, and what they think is practical is actually theory - usually, a bad theory; a faulty practice theory.

Practice theories are resolute ideas possessed by executives on how to think about and do things. They are inaccurate or completely incorrect theories that are partially or fully disconnected from reality (the practice ground). Faulty practice theories strongly influence management thinking and decision-making in that they enable wrong decisions and actions and disable correct decisions and actions.

Here are some examples of faulty practice theories related to both leadership and general management:

- Being zero-sum (win-lose) in decisions and actions has no unfavorable consequences. It is a free lunch.
- People (stakeholders) or organizations who have been marginalized will not try to get even.
- Management tools will fix any type of problem that one can encounter.
- It is appropriate to manage in the absence of business principles.
- Financial leverage greater than 10:1 is an acceptable risk.
- Decisions are correct simply because of one's high rank in the organization.
- What get measured gets managed.
- Must be success-oriented; focus on the upsides and downplay or ignore any downsides.
- Performance metrics are correct and helpful, and do not need to be questioned.
- Sharing with other stakeholders is bad.
- Management's job is to maximize shareholder value.
- If I find information that supports my idea, then my idea is a good one.
- I do not need to test my beliefs and assumptions.
- Organizational politics are a fact of life.
- Outsiders know more than internal company personnel.
- People understand what managers say.

Here are some examples of faulty practice theories specific to Lean management. Lean is:

- Only for manufacturing or operations.
- Tools for manager's tool kit.
- A way to cut costs.
- A method to improve quality and reduce lead-times.
- Something that workers to do, not leaders

- Sustainable after a few years of training and effort.

These faulty practice theories reflect an incurious and carefree perspective best described as "Bunga-Bunga" management. It is management practice disconnected from reality, unconcerned with cause-and-effect, short on facts yet long on opinion, and built on a foundation of willful ignorance, bad logic, and defective reasoning. This, unfortunately, is how educated leaders with decades of professional experience think about and practice management.

Business and management education, over 130 years old now, still has a long way to go before it produces high quality managers who are driven post-diploma to investigate and correct faulty practice theories.

As an educator, I am profoundly disappointed by those managers who, after they have finished their formal education, do not continue learning about their profession - particularly given its great importance to individuals and society.

Lesson 17

Ultimate Solutions

We know that Lean management requires dedication to continuous improvement to achieve steady progress, and to do so in non-zero-sum (win-win) ways so as not to marginalize the interests of key stakeholders (individuals and organizations) who are needed to successfully operate a business. The "Continuous Improvement" principle reflects the need to improve in response to new customer needs, new ideas, and changing circumstances over time. The "Respect for People" principle reflects the need to help ensure that improvements do not result in zero-sum outcomes - winners and losers. These two principles are practical and effective, and they force people to think in ways as never before.

What, then, do we do when senior managers, who long ago stopped thinking, believe that they possess ultimate solutions to common business problems (e.g. cutting pay and benefits, layoffs, plant closings, squeezing suppliers), or use ultimate solutions developed by others (e.g. simple mathematical equations such as economic order quantity, purchase price variance metric, learning curves, or economies of scale)? While they may be correct for batch-and-queue material and information processing, they are entirely wrong for flow. Through participation in kaizen, managers at all levels would learn to question their deeply-held ultimate solutions.

In order to progress, one must become enlightened. You do that by questioning what you and others think are ultimate solutions. You begin testing your realities - e.g. that batch-and-queue is the most effective way to organize resources for processing material and information - by applying the Scientific Method, just as Nicolaus Copernicus tested the then reality that the Earth was the center of the Universe. Kaizen, done right, is a practical application of the Scientific Method, and shows that workers, not managers, are the center of the business universe.

The quest for enlightenment can get you in trouble, as almost any change agent can attest. Organizational politics is a powerful force against change, no matter how true the new reality may be. We see this all the time with Lean management, as organizations seek to preserve as much of the old reality as possible by applying Fake Lean, which guarantees the continuation of zero-sum decisions, wasteful behaviors such as organizational politics and blame, and the wrong metrics. They will never achieve flow.

Rare is the leader, who, after many years of success, can acknowledge their fallibility and imperfections. While some may acknowledge a couple of minor faults, few would say they completely misunderstood the fundamental purpose of business, measured almost everything wrong, organized resources inefficiently, and supplied to customers products and services that were not as good as they could have been. Even rarer is the established CEO or president who can summon the energy to lead efforts to correct matters, learn new things, unleash human creativity in the organization, and give to customers what they deserve.

The problem is largely one of certitude. Leaders typically assume far greater knowledge than they should, for their own good and the good of their stakeholders. The words "close-minded" and "progress" do not go together. For a CEO or president to learn and lead Lean management, they must be open-minded and look for better solutions to all problems, and then keep looking for better solutions to those same problems and new ones. Forget about ultimate solutions or perfection because they discourage thinking and inhibit progress.

Business is a social science, which means the mathematics that describes the discipline, precise as it may seem, is an approximation of reality. Do not be fooled by the ubiquity of the equal sign (=) in equations. Ultimate solutions in business are very few in number, and everything can be improved. Want innovation? Then be open-minded and be progressive.

Lesson 18

Virginia Mason Visits Wiremold

On 5 November 2001, a group of more than 25 executives, physicians, and department managers from Virginia Mason Medical Center made the long trip from Seattle, Washington, to West Hartford, Connecticut, to take a tour of The Wiremold Company. Dr. Gary Kaplan, Chairman and CEO of VMMC, had come to see Lean management as the future of healthcare. The trip to Wiremold would help cement that view.

At that same time, I was leading a research project to write a book about The Wiremold Company's Lean transformation from 1991-2001. VMMCs visit to Wiremold coincided with the data-gathering phase of what later become the book, *Better Thinking, Better Results*. As part of the research project, I had all of the conference room presentations videotaped. The resulting 6 hours of recordings, plus over 800 pages of transcribed interviews, became the basis for the detailed description of Wiremold's Lean transformation contained in the book.

Since November 2011 is the 10th anniversary of that visit, I decided recently to watch the videos again. I had not seen them since early 2002, and I can tell you that I was very impressed with what I saw – from both the Wiremold executives and the VMMC team. The videos are a wonderful part of the history of both Lean management and Lean in healthcare.

Arthur Byrne, the president and CEO of Wiremold, welcomed any visitor to Wiremold as long as their CEO was present. For this visit, the CEO, Gary Kaplan, was more than just present. He was an active participant, eager to learn new things, and – very importantly – ready to put into practice what he had learned. The day consisted of factory tours and conference room meetings in which Art Byrne, Orest (Orry) Fiume (vice president finance and administration), Kevin Fahey (vice president of human resources), and others gave presentations. The presentations were highly interactive, with lots of good questions from the VMMC team.

Wiremold executives' deep knowledge of the nuances and details of Lean leadership and Lean management reflect a level of engagement in thinking about and actually doing Lean that is rare among executives. The videos reveal an engaged VMMC healthcare team that had no hang-ups about visiting an old factory to learn about Lean management. They made the jump from shop floor and office processes to medical procedures and healthcare administration, crossing a chasm that so many others in healthcare and elsewhere could not.

In the videos, the Wiremold executives do a wonderful job of translating Lean management from manufacturing to healthcare, and in doing so show how Lean can be applied to any organization in any industry. I have two key takeaways from the videos that I would like to share with you. They are:

- The Wiremold senior management team's determination to immerse themselves in daily Lean thinking and practice – for more than a decade – and willingness to share and help others; to teach others and to learn from others. These are typical characteristics of highly effective Lean leaders.

- The VMMC team members, CEO on down, were willing and eager to learn new things. They recognized that they were not educated or trained for Lean at any point in their careers. And yet they did not suffer from the typical "I'm the doctor, so don't tell me what to do" or "It won't work here because we're a hospital" mentality.

The Wiremold and Virginia Mason experiences inform us of the importance of a CEO who is committed learning and moving the organization forward. These examples are few, when there should be many. Are you up for the challenge?

Lesson 19

Becoming a Lean Leader

People who have seen the Wiremold videos have comment how they are amazed that a CEO is able to talk that way about Lean management. What Art Byrne says is completely different from anything they have ever heard from their own CEO. I agree. The most my former CEO could say about Lean was that it is "simply process mapping and process re-engineering."

When the top executive can speak like Art, then you know your Lean transformation is actually going somewhere. No more Fake Lean, at last. Art Byrne and his entire senior management team were able to talk about Lean that way in 2001 because they did far more than simply support Lean management, as my former CEO did and as nearly all others do. Instead, they learned Lean by doing, over the long-term, and they improved their understanding through ongoing thinking and practice. They understood that they were never done learning, unlike those executives who do nothing more than offer their support for Lean, and, in doing so, inform others that they were done learning long ago.

So, is that all there is to it: daily Lean thinking and practice? The answer is both "yes" and "no." "Yes," because to get good at anything requires an extraordinary amount of purposeful practice. Art and his team wanted to get good at Lean management because of its enormous strategic benefits, while other executives want to get good at different things. "No," because now, unlike 20 years ago, we understand the specific changes that occur in leaders' beliefs, behaviors, and competencies as a result of applying Lean principles and practices daily. These new beliefs, behaviors, and competencies must be better understood and practiced by leaders in order to achieve REAL Lean (see *Practical Lean Leadership* and *Moving Forward Faster*).

Sometime in late 2001 or early 2002, perhaps earlier, I realized that the changes executives undergo when applying Lean principles and practices daily is analogous to the process used to reduce change-over time for machine set-ups. This is not to say that managers are the same as machines, but to instead illustrate that the basic process is the same. I described this in Chapter 11 of *Better Thinking, Better Results*, the book about Wiremold's Lean transformation. The process to reduce machine change-over time consists of four steps:

1. Identify and separate internal and external set-up.
2. Convert internal to external.
3. Decrease internal set-up.
4. Combine and eliminate tasks to decrease internal and external set-up.

The process to change-over an executive's mind from batch-and-queue thinking to REAL Lean thinking is also a four-step process:

1. Recognize internal (tacit) conventional management beliefs and assumptions.
2. Convert internal (tacit) conventional management beliefs and assumptions to external (explicit).
3. Reduce internal (tacit) conventional management beliefs and assumptions.
4. Decrease internal (tacit) and external (explicit) conventional management beliefs and assumptions.

The late Bill Moffitt, who wrote the Foreword to *Better Thinking, Better Results*, had this to say about my model for how executives change over from batch-and-queue thinking to Lean thinking (page x):

> "Another thought-provoking and innovative chapter deals with a new way to look at the change process. By using the machine set-up reduction model to suggest ways by which senior leadership

> can achieve the required behavioral changes, Bob Emiliani sheds new light on the most critical aspect of the Lean transformation – the effectiveness of change management across the entire organization. It should give the executive reader much to ponder and act upon."

Indeed, it should. I have done a lot of work since *Better Thinking, Better Results* was written in 2002 to further understand and share with you the many nuances and details related to Lean management and Lean leadership. Yet my change-over model remains the simplest and most accurate representation of how to develop the required beliefs, behaviors, and competencies, and to be able to speak as Art Byrne did in 2001 about Lean management.

The fact that so few executives today can speak like Art Byrne tells you that they refuse to engage the change-over process and remain fully committed to batch-and-queue thinking or zero-sum Fake Lean. To simply offer support Lean is a near-worthless, empty management commitment because it does not result in the development of the beliefs, behaviors, and competencies characteristic of Lean leaders. As a result, they will never know Lean and will never be able to teach it to others. Instead, they will stand on the sidelines and self-limit their role to that of clumsy Lean cheerleaders.

The Wiremold (and Virginia Mason) story give current and aspiring leaders highly effective role models to learn from and emulate. I hope some will take advantage of that.

Lesson 20

Fair Business is Moral Business

Zero-sum (win-lose) outcomes, in which one party gains at the expense of another, are common in business, due in part to competitive pressures, time constraints, poor business school education, poor leadership, and a lack of critical thinking. The means by which to achieve non-zero-sum (win-win) outcomes is difficult to fathom, so nearly all senior managers ignore that choice and are satisfied with zero-sum outcomes in which they and the organization are the winner. In essence, they vigorously pursue shortcuts to get where they want to go, resulting in perceptions of unfairness. That is not the way things are done in REAL Lean management.

People have a basic expectation of fairness in their interactions with other people. This expectation also exists among people conducting business transactions because business is a socio-economic activity. The principle of fairness is accepted as a fundamental moral construct for human interaction. Therefore, outcomes in business that are unfair can be seen as immoral. However, that is usually not the case, as people can be very forgiving: an outcome is fair as long as it is not too unfair. But if unfairness goes beyond commonly accepted limits, or is seen as outrageous, then a judgment of immoral practices may be made.

The following three examples illustrate unfairness going beyond commonly accepted limits, which makes people upset and causes them to disengage or look for ways to get even.

The first example is the use of online reverse auctions (ORA), in which a buyer pits new and incumbent suppliers against one another in real-time dynamic bidding to drive down purchase prices. While ORAs may have a broader purpose than to drive down prices, rapid price reduction is the main focus and principal desired outcome from the buyer's perspective. The process is clearly zero-sum in its intent: suppliers' financial losses are buyers' financial gains. The use of ORAs has been so divisive that people have worked to soften the zero-sum outcomes for suppliers, such as introducing ORA codes of conduct – but to avail. ORAs are nothing more than technology-assisted zero-sum power-based bargaining. Suppliers soon realize there is nothing in it for them and refuse to participate.

The employees who run ORAs are caught between management's mandate for cost reduction and the company's ethics policies, which typically cite fairness as a fundamental requirement for how business will be conducted. Thus, management has put purchasing people into a position where they are forced to deviate from ethics policies, yet will surely be held accountable on an individual basis for failure to comply with ethics policies. That too is unfair – to one's own employees.

The second example is that of Fake Lean. Most organizations' Lean efforts are nothing more than a large-scale zero-sum effort to reduce costs. The rapid introduction of zero-sum Fake Lean is due to a combination of short-term thinking, ignorance of what Lean management is, and ineptitude on the part senior managers and consultants.

Nevertheless, the resulting zero-sum outcomes negatively impact one or more key stakeholders: employees, suppliers, customers, investors, and communities. The most common and most damaging outcome is to lay employees off as a result of process improvement. This quickly results in a tangible sense of unfairness that destroys employees' desire to participate in continuous improvement. It also fundamentally contradicts the "Respect for People" principle.

The cause-and-effect is obvious, yet managers choose to ignore this reality and continue to expect employees to participate in continuous improvement. Can this be seen as anything but unfair, and unreasonable? Note also that continuous improvement engineers are put in a position by management to cut costs by improving processes, which often means unemployment for their colleagues, yet also abide by the company's code of ethics – which will usually cite fairness as a fundamental requirement for how business will be conducted. This too is unfair to one's own employees. Fake Lean is unfair Lean.

The third and final example relates to corporate wealth; *creating* shareholder value, which is one of the responsibilities of senior management – not *maximizing* shareholder value. In the early 1970s, two U.S. business school professors wrote a paper in which they argued that granting stock options to top executives would compel them to think like owners and make decisions that better reflected owners' interests. The professors and others continued to advocate for changes in executive compensation as a means of improving decision-making and to increase shareholder value. Within about 10 years, the idea had begun to take hold in corporate boardrooms, and annual executive compensation for American executives went from about 90 percent cash salary and 10 percent stock options, to about 10 percent cash salary and 90 percent stock options. As might be expected, what has happened in the U.S. since the early 1980s is a never-ending stream of new tactics designed to increase stock price, usually at someone else's expense – most often employees.

The tactics are many and include: mergers, acquisitions (and usually overpay); lay people off (discretionary, automating tasks and jobs, etc.); stock buybacks (usually at peak prices, which consume the greatest amount of cash); eliminate defined benefits pension plans; cut wages; limit wage increases to 3 percent or less; cut current employee benefits; cut retiree benefits; underfund pension and benefits plans; take out life insurance policies on employees to fund deferred executive pay; use pension funds to finance retiree healthcare benefits; hire contractors to do the work formerly done by employees (thereby reducing headcount, wages, and benefits expenses); rapidly grow the company (to be so large through acquisitions that it cannot be managed effectively) then split it into two or more independent pieces; conduct online reverse auctions to reduce the purchase prices of goods and services; outsource work; offshore work to lower wage countries; hire cheaper labor (H-1B visa swizzle); increase dividend payments to investors.

Have I missed anything? Yeah, probably. How about creating shareholder value by improving the value proposition for end-use customers!

During the last 40 years, American workers' productivity has increased nearly as much as in the period 1947-1975, yet median real wages have steadily declined and household income has declined more than 10 percent since 2000. Despite all the merger and acquisition activity over the last 30 years, which has greatly reduced the number of competitors in most industries and increased market reach, most companies have little pricing power because workers' wages have decreased substantially. That, plus year-over-year increase in healthcare insurance premiums, forces companies to continue to cut costs via process improvement and outsourcing, both of which result in more layoffs. Thankfully, however, the stock price continues its upward march.

Note that leading economists want you to believe that technology and globalization are the two principal causes of income disparity, and thus greatly diminish the role of the aforementioned list of zero-sum tactics that have long been used by senior managers. Note also that flat wages and layoffs cause tax receipts to decline, which, in turn, lays the groundwork for privatizing public assets. This is how citizens unfairly lose their public assets.

What has emerged among U.S. workers over the decades is a sense of unfairness that has gone from tolerable to intolerable, resulting in discontentment and conflict. The actions taken to increase stock price have left the workers who add value to goods and services, and other stakeholders, behind. Is this the outcome that executives, who were incentivized to think and act as owners, wanted? Is that the outcome that actual business owners truly want?

REAL Lean business is moral business because it seeks to ensure that outcomes are fair – no perfectly so, but reasonably so. One party may not gain as much as it wants, but it does not lose as much as it could.

Perhaps the moment for Lean management to take off has finally arrived, but for a reason far different than anyone of us could have imagined: as an antidote to long-term systemic unfairness in business.

REAL Lean business is fair business.

Lesson 21

Atomized Kaizen

What has happened to kaizen? In my travels and conversations with people, kaizen is rarely practiced the way I learned it starting in 1994 from Shingijutsu consultants (who were mainly ex-Toyota and ex-Toyoda Gosei industrial engineers, supervisors, and managers). In many organizations, kaizen has mutated into a process that offers little in the way of the learning necessary to correctly understand and practice Lean management. Given the critical importance of kaizen to becoming a Lean leader, the changes that have occurred over the last decade are surely for the worse.

When we first did kaizen, we predominately used the week-long format (one of many formats, both shorter and longer). Each member of our cross-functional team was assigned a specific piece of current state data to gather on the Thursday and Friday prior to the kaizen. We collected the following information: cycle times, product-quantity analysis, process matrix, spaghetti chart, 5S evaluation, process-at-a-glance, time observations, takt time calculation, capacity study, established our goals, and created a target progress report to monitor daily progress.

We were not taught material and information flow analysis at the time (popularly known as "value stream maps"). If we were, we probably would have drawn only the current state map and used that sheet simply as just another piece of information. It would not have been the singular driving force behind kaizen (as it often is today), and I am certain we would have never drawn a future state map at the start of kaizen. Instead, we would have drawn the future state after we completed our kaizen. The future state was defined by two things:

- Achieve flow, principally by reducing batch size and by identifying and eliminating queues,

- The team's targets (not management's targets) as shown on our target progress report.

We then presented the current state data (various spreadsheets filled in by hand) and the kaizen team's targets to our sensei Monday morning. Sensei asked questions about our process, which we dutifully answered as best we could, and he adjusted our targets up or down to be more aggressive. Sensei then gave us some general direction on what to do, and off we went.

During the Monday-through-Friday part of our kaizen, we did the following: 5S (never 6s), time observation, operator percent loading charts, visual controls, standardized work and SWIP, standardized work combination sheets, installed safety and mistake-proofing devices, moved people and equipment, created skills matrix, and cross-training plans. We made major improvements daily and the team leader reported the results every afternoon at 4:30 pm to sensei, managers, and others (while team members continued their work). The final kaizen report-out was at noon on Friday, usually with zero action items remaining on our kaizen newspaper.

The kaizen I learned was rapid data gathering followed by focused thinking and doing – "doing," as in concentrating resources to get 100 percent of the improvements done quickly. It was the team's responsibility to think – to understand the current state and establish targets – and, with sensei's guidance, figure out how to improve process flow and meet or exceed the targets. Note also that support services (facilities, IT, purchasing, etc.) were available on-demand to immediately respond to anything that the kaizen team requested. Normal work request processes were suspended to assure that action items were completed quickly and did not linger undone for weeks to after the kaizen.

In addition, we did this type of kaizen every couple of weeks, not once every few months as I commonly see today.

These days, people do 5S "events," value-stream mapping "events," visual controls "events," standardized work "events," and so on. Each improvement is done separately, rather than combined, as I had learned. Often, these "events" are planning activities comprised of single-function (vs. cross-functional) team members. And, worst of all, they often result in recommendations to management for improvement. In other words, they have to get permission from management to make actual improvements. After a delay, management might give permission to proceed. However, improvements are often incomplete due to lingering action items. This is wrong! It is no way to do kaizen, and it is obviously inconsistent with the "Respect for People" principle.

In my experience, management understood there were mountains of waste, unevenness, and unreasonableness, and so we never had to seek permission to improve. We just did it. The disciplined kaizen process we used yielded great results in a short time, and we took pride in what we accomplished.

Kaizen, unfortunately, has been atomized into its component pieces as a means for management to maintain control over process improvement, force compliance to management's targets, and put limits on what management perceives to be a disruptive activity. While those objectives may be achieved, micromanaging kaizen reduces employee creativity, blocks information flows, and slows down improvement. This is no way to create a Lean enterprise. Nor does it result in the learning of Lean by managers to transform themselves into Lean leaders. Instead, we now have bad management on steroids.

Kaizen is the principal means by which senior managers learn about processes and how to improve them, and also – importantly – the nuances and details of Lean management. If they refuse to participate in kaizen or learn abnormal forms of kaizen, then they do not learn what they need to learn to become effective Lean leaders.

It is akin to learning to play six-string acoustic guitar, but with two strings, no sound hole, and a one-quarter octave, convex-bowed neck. To learn how to play guitar you need a normal guitar – not an abnormal guitar. To learn Lean management, managers (and employees) must learn normal kaizen.

Lesson 22

The Policy

I have long been concerned about the ease with which most (99 percent) managers misunderstand and incorrectly practice Lean management. This phenomenon goes back over 100 years and plagued the Scientific Management community as well. One particular problem stands out, then and now, that has severely limited the appeal of progressive Lean management to workers: layoffs. This is the all-too-common outcome that follows successful continuous improvement activities, and demonstrates management's utter disrespect for employees.

Viewing workers as disposable is anti-human and anti-family. It reflects a systematic devaluation of workers' knowledge. It reflects a view that people are always the problem. It reflects management's inability to lead and to develop the potential of the humans that they employ. What is the result of this view of employees on future progress.

After initial success, further continuous improvement becomes more difficult to achieve because the remaining people fear they might suffer unemployment as well. So, instead, we witness the appearance of continuous improvement as people game the processes, the metrics, the visual controls, the levels of Lean achievement, and so on. Remarkably, senior managers are almost universally oblivious to cause-and-effect and do not see the connection between continuous improvement and the need for people to feel safe and secure in their employment. Everyone realizes that nobody can guarantee a job for life, but no employee should have to fear loss of employment due to continuous improvement.

In all of my travels, I have rarely come across an organization where top management has given to workers at all levels a qualified job guarantee as they begin their Lean transformation:

"Nobody will become unemployed as a result
of continuous improvement activities."

Nor does management give employees a qualified job guarantee later on, to give them the basic safety and security that would motivate them to continue learning and improving. Instead, employees toil away to achieve many small, localized improvements because they are forced to do so, while system-level improvement does not occur. Executives, the employees learn, are easy to fool when it comes to continuous improvement because they do not know what to look for or because they look for the wrong things (e.g. pretty charts).

The actual outcomes achieved are far from what could be achieved were it not for an inability by generations of senior managers to comprehend one simple cause-and-effect relationship. Fake Lean is assured when employees are laid off as a result of continuous improvement, and that is indeed what we see in most organizations. We cannot expect better outcomes if this fundamental problem continues to exist.

Various organizations promote Lean management, including: Association of Manufacturing Excellence, Healthcare Value Leaders Network, Lean Enterprise Academy, Lean Enterprise Institute, The Shingo Prize, and many others in the U.S. and elsewhere. None of these organizations has a policy statement regarding their position on layoffs resulting from continuous improvement.

Both directly and indirectly, they have, for years, failed to point out to all interested parties the requirement for a qualified job guarantee and the criticality of the "Respect for People" principle (employees, as well as suppliers, customers, investors, and communities) in Lean management. Neither is optional. Yet we must also recognize the reality that senior managers in most organizations will be satisfied with zero-sum Fake Lean - even if they know better - and there is not much anyone can do about that.

So what would be a sensible and practical policy statement? How about this:

> "In support of our purpose to advance Lean management, we recognize two long- standing, inviolate principles, 'Continuous Improvement' and 'Respect for People,' and the requirement for their daily application by all senior managers. Fundamental aspects of the 'Respect for People' principle include assurance given by top management that no employee will suffer unemployment as a result of continuous improvement and the establishment of a 'no-blame' policy. Stakeholders (i.e. employees, suppliers customers, investors, and communities) shall no longer be treated in zero-sum (win-lose) ways because doing so severely disrupts material and information flows."

While policy statements may not do much to move senior managers towards REAL Lean, at least the customers of the organizations that promote Lean management will begin to learn that the "Respect for People" principle matters. Otherwise, there is little hope of doing any better than Fake Lean.

It is inconceivable that employees will accept Lean management if they are the ones who have the most to lose. When will we, the champions of Lean management, finally acknowledge this reality and make the "Respect for People" principle the central feature of our work - as opposed to just Lean tools?

If we do not, then history will be our trusted guide: Lean advocates will work hard for 20, 30, or 40 years and achieve almost nothing.

Think about that.

Lesson 23

Same Questions, Never Any Answers

You have to feel a lot of sympathy for employees, across a range of manufacturing and service industries, who, over the decades, have had to endure executive's insatiable appetite for improving financial performance at their expense. While managers may call what they are doing "Lean," the methods used – layoffs, outsourcing, closing plants and offices, etc. – bear no resemblance to REAL Lean management. These zero-sum (win-lose) actions appear in news headlines and instill fear in workers. They have decided against participating in improvement activities even before their managers have asked them.

Employees have expressed the same six principal criticisms of progressive management for over 100 years, across every industry sector and sub-sector that you can think of – manufacturing, service, non-profit, and government. From the perspective of workers, the value adders, progressive management is a major cause for concern because it will:

- De-humanize them
- Speed them up and burn them out
- De-skill them
- Take away their knowledge
- Take away their creativity
- Cost them their job

These six concerns matter to employees, and clearly inform us of what they consider very important aspects of not only their job, but their life. They are obviously worried about what they might lose and are not interested in management making gains at their expense. Given the proliferation of zero-sum Fake Lean in organizations over the decades, employees' concerns are fully justified.

The six principal concerns that employees have about progressive Lean management are well-known and consistent over time. Therefore, senior managers must be prepared to answer employees' questions about these six concerns. However, I have never heard of executives anywhere addressing these six concerns at the start of a Lean transformation. Nor have I heard them address these six concerns five, 10, or 20 years into a Lean transformation. How can one expect employee buy-in for Lean when management never responds to their most basic concerns?

Because management never addresses employee concerns, which is a "Respect for People" principle problem, they do not get anything more than perfunctory, check-the-box participation in continuous improvement. Management gets continuous improvement labor, but does not win employees' hearts and minds. The "Respect for People" principle activates the "Continuous Improvement" principle in Lean management. Ignore that connection at your own risk.

Workers have thoroughly criticized progressive management for 100 years, and will do so for the next 100, 200, and 300 years until executives address these six concerns. And, the only way to do that is to abandon zero-sum Fake Lean and embrace non-zero-sum (win-win) REAL Lean.

I was recently speaking to a large group of continuous improvement facilitators, many of whom were industrial engineers, and asked if anyone was familiar with Frank Gilbreth's pioneering bricklaying experiments from the late 1800s. Nobody was. Herein lies the key to explaining the six concerns that employees have always had about progressive management. Gilbreth's studies showed that bricklayers were not dehumanized, sped-up, or de-skilled, nor was their knowledge and creativity taken away. And, they did not lose their jobs.

Managers at all levels, as well as continuous improvement facilitators, must be able to explain Gilbreth's bricklaying experiments as one way to answer the many questions pertaining to employees' six concerns. This will help, at long last, to engage employees' hearts and minds in continuous improvement.

Lesson 24

Lean Management Failure at ________

It is truly spectacular to see a Lean transformation that goes well from the start, where people are involved and happy, processes are improved, and favorable business results are achieved.

Unfortunately, it is equally spectacular to see Lean efforts that fail as soon as they begin. The critical failure point invariably pertains to people – especially employees – who almost immediately suffer a wide range of zero-sum (win-lose) outcomes due to senior management's drive to quickly cut costs via process improvement. The trouble always revolves around the same set of key issues.

So, I have written a standardized article to describe the typical failed Lean effort. All I need to do to complete the article is fill in a few blanks to identify the organization in question. It is a great time-saver. But seriously, anyone who dislikes Lean management or thinks it is bad should read this Lesson.

• • • • •

The controversy and negative reaction surrounding the introduction and practice of Lean management at __________ is well-deserved given the flawed approach taken and the resulting terrible outcomes. It is clear that Lean management was not actually put into practice at __________. Management, driven by its consultant, unfortunately applied a highly degenerate and dysfunctional derivative form of new management practice that resulted in a proliferation of zero-sum (win-lose) outcomes. I have long called this "Fake Lean." A better name, perhaps, would be "No Lean."

It is far more common, by a factor of 500 to 1 or more, to witness the rapid emergence of zero-sum Fake Lean in organizations due to a combination of short-term thinking, ignorance of what Lean management is, and ineptitude on the part senior managers and consultants. The ability to discern the true intent of Lean management, and hence to practice it correctly, requires one to understand the history progressive management and its evolution over the last 100 years.

The forerunner of Lean management is Scientific Management. It too is much derided, until one realizes the true intent of its originator, Frederic Winslow Taylor. Taylor wanted to improve productive capacity for the good of workers (wage increases, less arduous work, and better trained workers), enterprises (sales growth and improved profitability), and the nation (GDP growth and international trade), and also improve cooperation between workers and management. He was specifically interested in eliminating disputes between workers and management which inevitably led to zero-sum outcomes. Taylor said the following words in testimony he gave to the U.S. Congress in January 1912:

> "It ceases to be scientific management the moment it is used for bad."

This statement captures Taylor's enormous frustration with how most senior managers and consultants mistakenly interpreted his work, as a fast way to achieve zero-sum outcomes that benefit the company at the expense of workers. The same frustration exists today for people who advocate Lean management. It too is seen by most managers and consultants as a fast way to achieve zero-sum outcomes that benefit the company at the expense of workers. Taylor's statement can be updated to characterize Lean management today:

> "It ceases to be Lean management the moment it is used for bad."

Lean management used for bad is not Lean management; it is simply bad management. This causes enormous headaches and confusion among managers and workers as to what Lean management really is. Being used for bad, one can only conclude that Lean management must be bad. But Lean is not bad in and of itself; this is a very important point to remember.

Unfortunately, zero-sum thinking is deeply ingrained among most senior managers and consultants, which is the principal way in which Lean is recognized as bad. Zero-sum thinking is so integral to management's mindset that senior managers simply do not understand how to achieve non-zero-sum (win-win) outcomes. It is a concept is so foreign to them that they ignore it all together. The approach to Lean taken at __________, and resulting outcomes, were thus entirely predictable.

Importantly, this same mistake is made over and over again by senior managers and consultants, despite having gained decades of practical knowledge that inform us of what to do and what not to do when introducing progressive Lean management into organizations. Consultants should know this, but apparently practicing progressive Lean management correctly does not generate sales to senior managers, most of whom are narrowly focused, time-constrained, and demand immediate cost savings.

Lean management is defined by two inviolate principles: "Continuous Improvement" and "Respect for People." These became principles of progressive Lean management because its foremost practitioners – Frederick Winslow Taylor (U.S., practice period ca. 1880-1914), Frank George Woollard (U.K., practice period ca. 1915-1933) and Taiichi Ohno (Japan, practice period ca. 1947-1978) – realized that you cannot have continuous improvement without respecting people. Importantly "people" in this context means an organization's stakeholders: employees, suppliers, customer, investors, and communities.

The "Continuous Improvement" principle expresses the need to improve on a daily basis in response to changing circumstances. The world changes every day, and so must we. At minimum, customers' expectations of quality and timeliness, for example, increase over time, and costs which increase inexorably must be leveled or reduced by improving processes – not by laying people off.

The "Respect for People" principle reflects the need to help ensure that improvements do not result in zero-sum outcomes - winners and losers. Taylor, Woollard, and Ohno were management practitioners, not academics, who each held positions in industry ranging from shop floor worker or engineer to senior executive as their careers matured. They learned from experience the importance of the "Respect for people" principle, and that it must not be seen by anyone – especially not by senior managers and consultants – as optional.

If the "Respect for People" principle is not recognized or is recognized but viewed as optional by senior managers, then failure is certain. The mistake that senior managers almost always make is to lay people off as the result of process improvement. That kills employees' desire to participate in continuous improvement and fundamentally contradicts the "Respect for People" principle. Is not the cause-and-effect obvious? Instead, people who have been made redundant must not lose their job and instead should be re-deployed to other areas of the organization to do productive work. This process is one of bilateral negotiation between employee, current manager, and future manager, to assure non-zero-sum outcomes. Workers are not the pawns of management in Lean, to be placed in jobs that are convenient for management but difficult for workers.

The "Continuous Improvement" and "Respect for People" principles are practical and effective, and they encourage people to think. And thinking is what Lean management requires, as it is often referred to as the "Thinking Management System." Managers have to think and they also must learn to trust workers to think. However, the outcome at __________ shows that neither the "Continuous Improvement" nor the "Respect for People" principles were understood, and thinking among managers was obviously on extended holiday. Taking the "No

Lean," zero-sum approach to process improvement to other sites will result in almost certain disaster.

What happened at __________ is a major failure that has negatively impacted many different stakeholders. It is too important a failure to quickly dismiss as the result of bad planning or bad execution, by blaming employees or suppliers (the consultants), or by scapegoating one or two high-level managers. The act of doing this, would, in itself, demonstrate that the "Respect for People" principle is not understood by __________ senior managers. There is no thinking going on here.

The cause of this failure should be carefully determined using formal root cause analysis such as by creating A3 reports. As senior managers at __________ are responsible for the failure, they must be the ones to think and learn from it by analyzing its root causes and identifying practical countermeasures in order to avoid future failures.

Importantly, failure analysis must not be used as yet another tactic to assign blame and it must not become politicized. It must instead be used as a means to identify process-related problems and to identify opportunities for process improvement. The failure analysis and countermeasures should be shared with other sites prior to their initiation of process improvement activities. If not, you can be assured that other sites will strongly resist any efforts to improve processes when outcomes for employees and other key stakeholders are certain to be zero-sum.

Now, the question one should ask is: Can the damage done at __________ be repaired? Yes, but it will require an ability to explain to __________ employees what Lean management is and how __________ efforts varied drastically from it in almost every way. Management will have to admit its mistakes and show the way forward to improve its Lean practice and achieve favorable outcomes. It is likely that some mid-level __________ managers are very frustrated by what happened and may also have a proper understanding of Lean management. I am sure they would love the opportunity to put their knowledge to use in leading efforts to help senior managers repair the damage. It will be very tough going, though, as employees do not easily give second chances to management.

As always, the weakness in senior management's efforts to introduce progressive Lean management into organizations is their lack of understanding of the "Respect or People" principle. They typically think they are already practicing this principle or that they know what it means. These are horribly faulty assumptions. If the "Respect for People" principle were easy to understand, including its inter-relationship with the "Continuous Improvement" principle, then Fake Lean would be rare and REAL Lean would be common. But REAL Lean – the daily application of both the "Continuous Improvement" and "Respect for People" principles – is rare while Fake Lean is, unfortunately, common.

The senior managers of __________ must realize that 100 percent of their university education and work experience pertains to non-Lean management. To emphasize this point, I tell people:

> "Don't confuse getting an 'A' or receiving
> a diploma with knowing anything."

That may seem harsh, but it is true. Formal education systems teach batch-and-queue information processing, while Lean seeks to achieve flow in information processing. The two are completely different fields of knowledge and practice, with almost no areas of overlap.

Therefore, to adopt Lean management means to learn something completely new. Senior managers, in particular, have a lot of homework to do gain a correct understanding of Lean management, which is a prerequisite for its correct practice. The bad news is that most senior managers are not eager to learn new things. The good news is that there are resources today that did not exist 10 or 15 years ago to help senior managers learn new things. The question is: Will senior managers be motivated to find and study those resources, put into practice what they learned, and make adjustments as their learning develops and improves over time? Or, will they simply blame someone for failure and move on?

Lesson 25

Business.xxx

In 1986, I saw the dark, mysterious David Lynch film, *Blue Velvet.* The most memorable lines were those uttered by Dennis Hopper's villainous character, Frank Booth. In one scene, he joyfully exclaimed: "Let's fuck! I'll fuck anything that moves," followed by a hideous laugh exposing malicious intent. Frank Booth, you see, was an "I win, you lose" kind of guy. Sometimes it seems as if Frank Booth's spirit lives vicariously in some corporations.

How so? Because a corporation is a debtor who often seeks to take advantage of its creditors – employees, suppliers, and communities – to gain something at their expense. It is true that in some cases the advantage sought is appropriate and within the bounds of good business practices and fair competition. But, in many cases they are not. In addition, certain zero-sum (win-lose) practices repeated often can become accepted as routine over time, even though they do not reflect good business practices nor advance fair competition.

Publications such as *The Wall Street Journal* contain articles every day that describe zero-sum, win-lose outcomes. These stories are far more newsworthy than non-zero-sum (win-win) outcomes. Indeed, some zero-sum outcomes are so striking that they draw the interest of government regulators and prosecutors for potential violations of law.

Let's look and see how this breaks down by each stakeholder category, using some representative examples of zero-sum actions.

- Employees: unpaid labor or unfair pay; elective layoffs; cutting benefits.

- Suppliers: delaying, avoiding, or cutting payments; debiting suppliers' accounts; requiring "pay to play;" squeezing suppliers margins (reverse auctions).

- Community: underpayment of taxes or royalties; plant and office closings; tax evasion or reincorporating offshore; damaging the environment.

Here we have debtors imposing debt forgiveness upon their creditors. Usually, it is the other way around – creditors grant debt forgiveness to debtors.

Some of these zero-sum actions may be acute, while others are chronic in many organizations. Regardless, they are simply unilateral efforts by debtors (buyers) to take advantage of creditors (sellers). Buyers seek debt forgiveness from sellers, ranging from a few percent to 100 percent, even in good economic times. Debtors act as if creditors are complete strangers whom they will never see again after the desired zero-sum economic transaction is completed.

Sometimes customers do not fare much better than creditors, as debtors may engage in price fixing and bid rigging, underpayment, tying agreements, differential treatment (throttling), overcharging, and extra or hidden fees.

Likewise investors, another key stakeholder, find that debtors sometimes do things that hurt their interests such as inflating earnings (i.e. expense & revenue recognition), hiding debt; channel stuffing; insider trading, and gaming stock options (e.g. back-dating).

Normalizing zero-sum thinking is bad for business. Frank Booth, however, would absolutely love this stuff because it is a fuck-fest. Anything that moves, anytime. Relationships do not matter. Key business stakeholders are just instruments to bargain with and to take advantage of whenever possible. Everyone does it, so why not me?

Managers can get into a lot trouble when their zero-sum actions are discovered, no longer tolerated by creditors, or used to misrepresent the financial condition of the company. If senior managers and the company's good name want to stay out of trouble and stay out of the news, then it is better for them to be non-zero-sum in their business dealings with their creditors, as well as customers and investors. Doing so is just not newsworthy.

Lesson 26

Great Lean Leaders

The following are typical characteristics of great Lean leaders, all of which are learned through daily practice and exposure to different work experiences.

- Reads and studies: A life-long learner. Wants to try out what they have learned.
- Curious: Likes to experiment and try new things. Not afraid to get their hands dirty.
- Asks why: Questions everything.
- Modest and unassuming: Not showy. Never says, "I already know that" or "I'm beyond that."
- Observes: Carefully observes people and processes. Focuses on process and results.
- Personally involved: Learns by doing and leads by example (servant leader).
- Persistent: Failure is not a barrier. Failure is a learning opportunity.
- Never stops thinking: Problems are a personal challenge.
- Never stops communicating: Likes to listen and teach others.
- Consistent: Devoted to development of self and others. Lots of self-discipline.
- Digs into things: Wants to understand problems, details, root causes, etc.
- Non-blaming, non-judgmental: Realizes that blaming people and judging people is waste.
- Supportive: Likes to help people. Sets people up to succeed. Does not think people are the problem.
- Pragmatic: Alert to problems caused by management certitude and overconfidence.

Observation of capable Lean leaders reveals a mindset that can be accurately characterized as follows:

The Way of Great Lean Leaders

Continuous Improvement Requires Respect for People

Respect for People Requires Having a Process Focus

Having a Process Focus Requires Thinking and Analysis

Thinking and Analysis Requires Asking Why

Asking Why Requires Curiosity

Curiosity Requires Humility

Humility Means Not Thinking You Know it All

As you can see, an open mind is the first step in the process of becoming a capable Lean leaders. The next step is a willingness to learn Lean principles and practices through hands-on work.

Lesson 27

Classroom v. Real World

Most people associate university professors, books they have written, and classroom teaching with theory. This perception may be accurate for professors who have had no actual long-term business experience in the knowledge areas that they teach. Unfortunately, this is often the case because the reward system in higher education strongly favors theory over practice. It also favors career academics, versus those with deep industry experience and who possess appropriate academic credentials.

Full-time professors with significant industrial experience typically approach their academic work very differently compared to professors with no industrial work experience. Their industry work experience infuses their teaching with practical knowledge learned. In my case, I literally cannot think of anything - any new idea, method, or practice - without first putting it into the context of the actual workplace; the hectic pace, interpersonal and interdepartmental relationships, meetings, budgets, etc. All of the books and papers that I have written have had this in mind.

Unfortunately, when most managers see a paper in an academic journal or a book written by someone with a Ph.D., they tend to think it is theory and therefore useless. (Note: what the Ph.D. really teaches is how to do research, think logically and factually, and write. These are practical outcomes which are of great importance to industry, even though the subject of some Ph.D. theses may be entirely theoretical). Senior managers with pressing day-to-day concerns and challenging targets to achieve do not read what they should to improve their understanding and practice of their chosen profession: management. That is too bad, because information that could be very helpful to them is often totally ignored.

So, not every professor, book, or classroom experience should be thought of as "theory." In fact, if you think back to your best professors, they were probably few in number, had significant industrial work experience, and likely held management positions. That is why my students, ranging from young adults to seasoned working professionals, think I am practical writer and practical teacher. Nevertheless, I always look for ways to improve, and especially in relation to helping students analyze real-world problems more broadly and to connect the dots.

Others in higher education seek to improve as well. In an article in *The Wall Street Journal* titled "Columbia's Business Dean on Disclosure, Leading, Ethics," the Dean of Columbia University's business school, R. Glenn Hubbard discussed how he is leading efforts to improve M.B.A. education. Hubbard, a former chairman of the President's Council of Economic Advisors, discussed how decision-making and ethics are being integrated into every course rather than taught as stand-alone courses as in other business schools. That sounds like good practical improvements in light of the recent financial crisis.

Hubbard said that first year M.B.A. students read a case "…on General Motors because GM's problems really did unfold over a 20- to 25-year period. It enables students to spot slow-moving train wrecks…" Later in the article, Hubbard said that to be a successful leader, one of three things they must do is analyze problems: "First, you've got to be able to analyze a problem. And that, frankly, almost any good business-school student can do."

Do you see the problem here? GM was led for nearly 50 years prior to its Chapter 11 bankruptcy in 2009 by business school grads with decades of (usually finance) experience who were unable (unwilling?) to analyze problems and put the brakes on their own slow-moving car wreck. A simple current state value stream map, depicting batch-and-queue processing, will show that most managers, M.B.A. or not, are awful at analyzing practical business problems.

What students can do in the classroom is, of course, far different from what they do in business. Good grades in college and graduate school fool most students into thinking they know something, which significantly reduces their desire to question things and leads to greater risk-taking than is warranted. Grading in graduate business school programs should be pass/fail, in part to strip away any indications of the level of excellence achieved and to promote continued questioning and prudent risk-taking after graduation.

In addition, as *The Wall Street Journal* article notes, many businesses school grads are placed in leadership roles with significant responsibilities very early in their careers. It seems that the odds of faulty decision-making and ethical lapses will be much higher in the future compared to those who gained the deep learning and reflection that comes from slowly practicing one's trade over time.

Business and management education have a long way to go before they produce managers who are as good in the real world as they were in the classroom.

Lesson 28

Fake Lean in Government

I think most of us would like to see progressive REAL Lean management in government, at all levels - local to federal, for reasons such as lowering the cost of government, improving existing services, supplying new services that taxpayers demand, and eliminating queues to improve flow. It is an appealing prospect, one that I have written about in my books, *REAL LEAN* Volume One ("Lean Government - Crazy Dream or Absolute Necessity"), *REAL LEAN* Volume Six ("Leanpolitik" and "Lean Without Thinking"), and *Moving Forward Faster.* Then there is reality.

In these books, I point out the many challenges of getting REAL Lean management into government, where the Scientific Method is at odds with the political method. For example, you will have to get conservative political leaders, who detest anything progressive, to accept progressive Lean management. Politically, conservatives will almost always accept Fake Lean (only the "Continuous Improvement" principle), just as conservative business leaders long have, but which results in widespread zero-sum (win-lose) outcomes that negatively affect key stakeholders - and always causes a loss of support for Lean, especially among workers.

More importantly, what will conservative politicians do when they are attacked as being a progressive for supporting Lean management? This is a fundamental, practical problem, because Lean management is firmly rooted in the Progressive era and with progressive-minded managers. There are many challenges for liberals and libertarians as well. Almost everyone struggles to understand work activities as processes and flow, compared to work activities performed in isolation via batch-and-queue.

I also discuss a legislative effort to mandate Lean in Connecticut State government and the difficulty of getting that right. In addition to the analyses in my books, I suggest numerous practical actions that will be needed to successfully introduce REAL Lean in government. To do this, you will need a really good plan. Without such a plan, the best you can hope to get is dis-continuous improvement. That's no good.

Mr. Michael George, a former consultant, is the head of Strong America Now. He has a plan, a rather poor plan, to introduce Lean Six Sigma in the U.S. federal government, which includes a pledge for politicians to sign. Mr. George's web site explains what is Lean Six Sigma (accessed 8 December 2011), and that is what I would like to discuss here. Parts of the explanations are paraphrased below, in bold, followed by my commentary. I do this to illustrate various misunderstandings about Lean management that have long existed, and which will surely undercut well-intentioned efforts to introduce Lean management to improve government services.

Lean is a process efficiency methodology for continuous improvement.

Lean is a management system, not a process efficiency methodology. Continuous improvement operates as both a principle and a process in Lean management; the process being kaizen, which can take many forms. There is no mention of the two principles of Lean management, "Continuous Improvement" and "Respect for People," nor the requirement for non-zero-sum (win-win) outcomes to help sustain continuous improvement. Therefore, Lean Six Sigma is a defective derivative of REAL Lean management narrowly focused on cost cutting and (mostly) one-time process improvement.

Lean focuses on the elimination of waste using Lean tools.
In Lean management, unevenness and unreasonableness are as important as waste. This narrow view of simply eliminating

waste, and the ease with which waste is eliminated, is misleading. Local efficiency improvements made using a few Lean tools are usually unsustainable and do not connect processes to achieve flow. Also, the application of tools alone, in the absence of the Lean management system framework, typically leads to zero-sum (win-lose) cost cutting which marginalizes key stakeholders. It is wrong to think of Lean as nothing more than a set of tools and techniques. Importantly, Lean management was developed to grow and improve a business (or organization), not for negative cutting.

Lean traces its origins to the 1950s.

Lean management's development has been evolutionary, beginning with Fredrick Winslow Taylor and his colleagues who created industrial engineering (and also Frank and Lillian Gilbreth) in the 1870s through the 1900s; Charles Sorensen and Henry Ford who established flow on the Model T production line in the 1910s and 1920s; Frank Woollard at Morris Motors, Ltd. in the 1920s; and Kiichiro Toyoda followed by Taiichi Ohno at Toyota in the late 1940s through the 1970s. Kaizen is the application of basic industrial engineering methods and good human relations practices to identify and correct process problems. Its origins are from the U.S. government's Training Within Industry (TWI) program introduced to Japanese industry after World-War II. TWI, of course, was based on Frederick Taylor's work, which, fundamentally, was to apply the Scientific Method to management of processes and improve cooperation between management and workers.

The terms lead-time and cycle-time are interchangeable.

These terms are not interchangeable. Cycle time is the time to complete one cycle of an operation. Lead-time is the total elapsed time between when a customer places an order to when they receive the product or service. Confusion between lead-time and cycle time is a typical consultant's error. There is no mention of takt time, the rate of customer demand, which is of great importance in Lean management.

Lean Six Sigma uses Lean tools to eliminate waste and Six Sigma to improve quality.

Lean is a management system, while Six Sigma is a quality improvement tool useful only under narrow circumstances. The two are not comparable. Lean people would not be interested in Six Sigma because it requires specialists, and continuous improvement will therefore be paced by the capacity of the specialists. In Lean, you want everyone to be able to identify a problem, determine its root causes, and identify and implement practical countermeasures – not just specialists. Lean and Six Sigma do not belong together. Also, most managers mess up Lean without Six Sigma, so why make Lean more complicated by adding Six Sigma? This is a big mistake.

I should also note that Mr. George's approach for training political leaders is well known to result in support for continuous improvement, but it does not result in their daily participation in continuous improvement. Without daily practice, they will never understand Lean management.

The outcome of Mr. George's plan will be Fake Lean in government. It is like building a bridge that you know will almost surely fail and hurt people. Fake Lean will cause much confusion and distress among workers and other key stakeholders such as taxpayers, and will likely have great difficulty surviving two-year election cycles, political appointee turnover, and basic investigative reporting.

Lean management was not designed for the political cauldron of government, where incentives for elected officials are greatly misaligned with the interests of government's stakeholders. You no longer focus on what is important to the customer and getting the job done they want you to do for them. REAL Lean management works only in environments with little or no politics because politics itself creates vast amounts of waste, unevenness, and unreasonableness. Politics, the art of appearance, is the antithesis of Lean, which is fact-based (i.e. Scientific Method). Debilitating conflict between the two is unavoidable.

In order to improve via Lean management, one must accept the Scientific Method, develop an accurate understanding of its principles and practices, and learn how they relate to each other to ensure good technique and thoughtful execution. One must also think through the problems one will encounter to avoid that which has a high probability for failure, such as aligning 535 elected officials in Congress and legions of political appointees and career civil service managers. If this is not done, then the result will be localized zero-sum efficiency initiatives scattered throughout government, large variation in the application of tools, and stifling bureaucratic oversight. These will assure that efforts to improve government services will be largely one-time and short-lived.

Mr. George's Strong America Now campaign, while laudable in its intent, shows that people, even those with considerable real-world experience, still do not understand Lean management. This is not a "Lean purist" perspective, but rather an entirely practical perspective to help assure good, long-term outcomes. There is little potential for improving the public sector (in fact, versus in appearance) if we do not apply the extremely valuable lessons that we have learned from the private sector for the last 100-plus years. We know what works and what does not, so let's put that knowledge to use and develop a better plan.

Lesson 29

Leadership Variation

Every semester I teach a graduate-level course in Lean leadership as part of our Master of Science in Technology Management degree program. Nearly all of the students are full-time working professionals who are pursuing their graduate degree part-time. Most are in their 30s or 40s with more than a decade of work experience. They typically have supervisory or mid-level management responsibility, and have had between five and ten bosses over the years.

In this course, we discuss leadership in ways that are substantially different than other leadership courses. Among the differences are to understand leadership as being made up of many different processes, all of which must be operated under non-steady-state conditions (i.e. in dynamic, changing times). Understanding leadership from a process perspective is non-existent in higher education. Instead, leadership is normally taught according to different academic theories of leadership. My approach is far more practical.

Initially, students struggle to understand leadership from a process perspective. They perceive leadership to be an ad hoc assortment of daily activities, even when the specific roles and responsibilities of leaders are fairly well defined. They generally accept this because they empathize with the time and job pressures that their managers face. While they certainly do not like poor leadership, they feel there is not much they can do to change it. The broader, chaotic business system drives their leaders to not lead.

The process perspective has distinct advantages in that it does a far better job helping students comprehend leadership. It also helps them realize that leadership is not the domain of the few people who possess unique personal characteristics such as charisma. Almost anyone can become an effective Lean leader.

The process perspective also helps students to do a better job of evaluating leadership quality and effectiveness. They recognize the variation in how leaders operate processes that are common among them. Note that a leadership team would be intolerant of a work team where each individual operated the process differently. Yet there is little or no actual requirement placed on a leadership team to operate their common processes with little variation.

The variation that students identify is often dramatic and contributes greatly to perceptions of poor leadership. This makes it difficult for them to do their job and is a great source of daily frustration. In addition, if the quality of fundamental processes is chronically low, then acute circumstances requiring intelligent, accurate, and strong leadership are likely to be absent.

Naturally, the process perspective of leadership leads to a discussion of the processes leaders engage in that can be standardized. Below are some processes that my students would like to see standardized in order to improve leadership quality, reliability, and effectiveness:

- Decision-making
- Meetings
- Communication
- Follow-up
- Feedback
- Performance reviews
- Employee development
- Career planning
- Training
- Hiring
- Resource allocation

Every organization has processes for each of these, be they informal or formal. Despite this, the processes normally vary widely in quality and the time it takes to complete them – even if the process has been formalized, as is usually the case in large organizations.

There is one important difference between these leadership processes and the value-creating work processes that occur at lower levels in the organization: the presence of organizational politics. Imagine if organizational politics generated at lower levels heavily influenced value-creating work. It is certain that very little work would actually get done. Instead, people would fight with each other, focus their attention on the wrong things, and waste a lot of time. Left unchanged, the company would soon go out of business. Fortunately, leaders do not directly engage in value-creating work processes, so work does actually get done: goods and services are provided to customers on a timely basis and cash is received by the company.

Left out of value-creating activities, leaders do other things (often, busy-work such as meetings). Many will become deeply involved in organizational politics, which simply adds cost but creates no value. (This is one big reason why all senior managers should participate in kaizen). This will surely make life more difficult and slow down every person and every process. Why is this a problem?

It is a problem because to standardize the work that leaders do, and thus improve leadership, means that organizational politics has to be greatly reduced, if not substantially eliminated. This is not as difficult to do as one might think, once senior managers recognize that organizational politics generates mountains of waste, unevenness, and unreasonableness. Politics is a major distraction that greatly impairs an organizations' ability to respond to customers and to changes in the marketplace.

Let's look at one example that affects us all: performance appraisals. What kinds of defects or quality problems can occur in a performance appraisal process?

- Inconsistent application
- Variation in interpretation of appraisal criteria
- Unclear expectations
- Intimidating
- Non-constructive feedback
- Biased appraisals (halo, leniency, similarity, central tendency, recency)
- Ego-driven decisions
- Lack of fairness
- Frequently re-scheduled
- Late
- Not completed
- Pay/bonus not tied to performance

It is apparent that there are many opportunities for leaders to make errors in just this one process, which will certainly lead to dissatisfaction among followers. The practical outcomes for employees can be increased stress, reduced motivation, and higher turnover.

Imagine all the errors that occur in each of the leadership processes listed previously. A key takeaway for you should be that leadership is an error-prone activity whose quality is normally very poor. This is at odds with our customary view of leadership as intelligent, thoughtful, and capable.

As the saying goes, "There is so much opportunity for improvement." I have long thought this to be an unfortunate saying because it reveals a chronic lack of attention by senior managers to process and outcomes. Even organizations that claim to be good at continuous improvement are usually unaware of the enormous variation in leadership processes and therefore tolerate poor quality and inconsistency among its leaders.

Where is HR in all of this?

Lesson 30

Relative Success, Absolute Failure

Like me, I am sure you have heard or experienced examples of organizations claiming success with Lean management. However, if get into the details, you find out what is really going on, and it goes something like this: Continuous improvement becomes bureaucratized and people play games to give the appearance of success. While there are many improvements, they are usually isolated from one another and flow is never achieved. And, senior management is clueless about or indifferent to the "Respect for People" principle.

Such organizations have accomplished nothing special. They have done what legions of others have done before them: Fake Lean. In relative terms, Lean has been a big success, and that is what outsiders typically see. When viewed in absolute terms, we see that their efforts have largely failed. And we know why; management did not lead, and people fear Lean. Here are ten comments from people whose organizations are highly regarded by knowledgeable outside observers for their Lean success (edited for clarity and brevity):

1) "When we have a kaizen, we don't focus on the activity, but rather the outcome. The improvements being made are outcome oriented because everyone is focused on reaching the goals of the organization. We do kaizen is to improve the metrics. After a kaizen, managers never fully allow the changes made to take effect."

2) "In our firm, kaizen is an event. We have remote islands of improvement. The company tends to promote itself, not the customer and thinks kaizens should be results oriented, not process oriented. The same is true of quality. There is a tendency for profit first, not quality first. Our balanced scorecards tend to be balanced towards profits, not the

customer. There is also a tendency to replace suppliers rather than do kaizens to help them improve things. Where there are large issues there is a tendency to seek home runs rather than incremental improvement."

3) "My company largely ignores the respect for people principle. There are strained relations between employees and managers. There is a mentality where managers always win and employees lose. Managers feel that employees are there to serve them. Strategy deployment is driven by the top with no involvement from lower levels. It's all about the metrics. This atmosphere causes people to live down to expectations. Managers do not have confidence in employees. One of the greatest areas of disrespect is towards suppliers. They are asked to do great things, yet we cannot do these things ourselves. They insist on top performance when the things they designed are very difficult to produce. These behaviors create confusion, strife, defensiveness, and poor communication, making relationships ineffective. There is a lack of mutual respect."

4) "My senior managers have little comprehension of what kaizen is and how to apply it. Their knowledge is mostly theoretical and most have never actually been involved in kaizen. Kaizen is conducted much like a focused improvement group which are assembled only when an issue arises. Kaizen is reactionary to address known problems, not used to prevent problems. It appears that managers have picked what they deem to be the most important aspects of Lean and forgotten the rest of the system."

5) "The respect for people principle is not understood at my company. The greatest failure of the principle comes in the form of layoffs and outsourcing. Once a kaizened process achieves a certain level of quality and reliability, it becomes a candidate for outsourcing. The fact that management does not have respect for people severely stifles the continuous improvement processes. CI is seen as a major negative force

at work. I don't believe that upper level management is fully committed to it and/or they don't really understand it."

6) "Kaizen events happen sporadically to address larger areas of concern. They are not used as part of a continuous improvement process. We were forced to participate in X number of kaizens to obtain certifications. They only use the tools selectively. The politics at work are a strong force. One thing is for sure, they don't really buy into the whole Lean philosophy, only the parts they want to."

7) "Most of the decision-making is centered on quarterly financial results which by its nature will undercut any momentum towards behaviors that promote trustworthy relationships between managers and employees. Lean tools/processes have been force-fit into the traditional management framework. It is more of a burden than a new way of managing to free-up employee creativity."

8) "It is the understanding of senior management that kaizen is to be delegated down to their subordinates. This is quite obvious because I have been involved in many kaizens and never have I witnessed a senior manager become involved."

9) "Where I work, respect for people is an afterthought at best. Management often looks at workers like numbers. If they could find a way to completely outsource the work, they would."

10) "I never hear about them [top managers] doing anything to improve their processes. I guess when you get to the top you don't have to work as hard to try and improve because you already reached the ceiling."

Remember, these organizations are highly regarded by knowledgeable outside observers for their Lean success. The key words are "outside observers." They can see only the façade of Lean management.

This is what success typically looks like in relative terms – particularly in organizations that are strongly controlled by finance.

The colorful charts that track continuous improvement, cost savings, and levels of Lean achievement in these organizations prove success and give the appearance to outsiders of dedicated and skilled work. Yet holding these organizations up as examples of success teaches that it is acceptable for senior managers to misunderstand Lean and practice it the wrong way.

This comment exemplifies incorrect understanding and practice of Lean management:

> "My company has a database for all of the projects, and it actually lets you declare how many jobs could be eliminated."

Managers who inadvertently or purposefully ignore the "Respect for People" principle are actually saying to employees:

> We don't actually want you to think, try new things, or experiment. We really don't care about teamwork, we don't care about flow, and we certainly don't care about you.

I do not see dedicated and skilled work here. What I see is casual and sloppy work, leading to absolute failure. Senior managers have made numerous beginners errors that immediately resulted in the creation of Fake Lean. Worse yet, they never even try to correct their beginner's errors. That is severely at odds with most executives' ego and desire for world-class performance. Errors left uncorrected doom one mediocrity. That is what happens when you think you are done learning.

To be educated means to be well-read. Then comes daily practice, to learn.

Lesson 31

Meaningless Victory

These pioneers of progressive management – Frederick Taylor, Frank Woollard, and Taiichi Ohno – have taught us much. However, we have not learned all the lessons that we can from them. Far from it. In fact, we have yet to learn their most important lessons, one of which is the predisposition of senior managers to cherry-pick tools and methods developed by the pioneers to achieve short-term gains. This lesson was ignored, and so history has repeated itself.

We all agree that Lean tools and methods are very important, but we have yet to come to grips with the fact that with just the tools and methods, the best one can hope to achieve is more efficient batch-and-queue processing. Zero-sum (win-lose) outcomes will be prevalent, and flow, which requires much more than just tools and methods, will never be achieved. There is now a common view that Lean has realized some significant, albeit limited, success. Namely, that "We've won the battle of ideas on how to operate and improve processes." Meaning, people broadly recognize that the tools and methods work and many people use them.

This was not, in fact, a battle, and there was nothing to win (but lots to lose). Managers hungry for better results have always gobbled up new tools and methods to improve productivity and cut costs. They love that stuff. The "We've won the battle…" characterization is off the mark and conceals the reality of our situation. Lean practitioners must always see reality as it is, to help assure that the PCDA problem-solving cycles they engage in reflect the right problem to work on.

The best that can be said regarding the spread of Lean tools and methods since the early 1990s is that we have not lost ground. However, it would be more accurate to say that we have actually lost substantial ground. If there was a battle in our era, we surrendered on day one sometime in the late 1970s. The battle, therefore, has yet to begin. Yet we have lost precious time and a huge amount of goodwill among the employees due to widespread zero-sum Fake Lean. Organizations rely on workers to recognize and solve problems every day, which they will not do if harmed by Lean.

The tools and methods used to improve productivity and reduce costs are to executives what salt, fat, and sugar are to dieters: irresistible temptations, but which can also cause great harm.

Throughout the history of modern progressive management, executives have cherry-picked the tools to achieve short-term gains, usually at the expense of employees, suppliers, and communities. The pioneers were very troubled by this.

Frederick Taylor and his team were frustrated that executives did not adopt the Scientific Management system in its full form. Instead, they used only the parts they felt were appropriate to their current needs. There was also rivalry and bitterness between Taylor's team and the legions of consultants that sprang up overnight claiming expertise, and who were very successful in selling senior managers only the tools of Scientific Management. Among their biggest concerns were that improvements would be short-lived and the consistently negative outcomes experienced by employees.

Frank Woollard had this to say about the importance of achieving non-zero-sum (win-win) outcomes for employees and other key stakeholders (*Principles of Mass and Flow Production*, p. 180):

> "Unless the eighteenth principle is satisfied the [flow production] system cannot reach full stature…This principle of 'benefit for all' is not based on altruistic ideals – much as these are to be

> admired – but upon the hard facts of business efficiency."

Taiichi Ohno experienced the cherry-picking phenomenon first-hand when he introduced Toyota's production system to Toyota's suppliers in the early 1970s (*NPS: New Production System*, p. 153, 155):

> "Companies make a big mistake in implementing the Toyota production system thinking that it is just a production method. The Toyota production method won't work unless it is used as an overall management system… those who decide to implement the Toyota production system must be fully committed. If you try to adopt only the 'good parts', you'll fail."

The pioneers of progressive management saw their work as a battle to replace conventional zero-sum management in its entirety with a non-zero-sum progressive management system. That must be our battle too.

We still have much to learn from the successes and failures of these pioneers, who worked so hard to establish progressive management in organizations on a broad basis. Shame on us if we ignore them and claim a meaningless victory.

Lesson 32

Work Towards A Higher Standard

Recognizing that REAL Lean is very difficult for managers to do, many Lean advocates are happy to see any process improvement in companies and organizations, in part to improve their own experiences as customers. I have long rejected that notion – not as an idealist, but as a pragmatist. While the processes may have been improved and waste eliminated, Fake Lean means that workers and other stakeholders will be exposed to unevenness and unreasonableness.

As a customer, I am not happy when continuous improvement results in layoffs. Should we, as customers, support businesses and organizations whose approach to continuous improvement is zero-sum (win-lose)? Should we praise the speeches or books about Lean journeys that regularly lay people off as a result of continuous improvement? Should we, as Lean advocates, ask their representatives to speak at Lean conferences? Should educators use their case studies in the classroom as exemplars of continuous improvement? I think not.

We should instead praise those few who correctly understand and practice Lean management, and, based on facts, criticize the many who do not and offer to help them improve.

A person who is laid off as a result of continuous improvement is someone's spouse, brother or sister, son or daughter, and who likely has been made miserable by their job loss – both a loss of daily purpose in life and a sudden loss of cash flow upon which one's life depends. It is not the role of management to make employees miserable. We need to help executives improve their understanding of Lean management so that they abandon zero-sum thinking and shun zero-sum outcomes.

So, this begs the question: Is some continuous improvement better than no continuous improvement? If the continuous improvement is zero-sum, then the answer, in my view, is "no." If the choice is my inconvenience versus someone becoming unemployed due to continuous improvement, then I would rather be inconvenienced (all other things being equal). The mistakes made today were perhaps reasonable ones to make 25 years ago when the "Respect for People" principle was not recognized – mainly because managers were blind to cause-and-effect. We now know better and we must do better as well. It is not right to praise organizations that have as their policy to reward people who improve processes by laying them off.

Perhaps the one positive thing that can be said about batch-and-queue material and information processing is that it is a full-employment system. However, that is not a good enough reason to continue using the batch-and-queue processing method. We must advance the practice of management but cannot get to Fake Lean and call that good enough.

Top executives repeatedly claim to want world-class performance, yet set the bar very low for themselves when they refuse to do any better than Fake Lean. We have accepted this for decades, but I believe we can no longer afford to be so generous.

If you, in your role as a Lean leader, are not advancing non-zero-sum REAL Lean every day – and everyone knows that is difficult and often very risky to do – then why bother? Continuing to proliferate zero-sum Fake Lean, the lower standard, will eventually kill Lean management.

Lesson 33

Micro Lean

After decades of observation and study, it is clear that Lean transformations must be led by CEOs. Yet we have a fundamental problem: Few CEOs are willing to learn something new that challenges their views of just about everything. Therefore, few CEOs can actually lead a Lean transformation. The best that some CEOs can do is to tell people to eliminate waste, while the remaining CEOs have zero interest in Lean management.

It would be great if all CEOs understood Lean and led the way to a more enjoyable and prosperous future for all key stakeholders. But this is not our reality, and we must accept this severe limitation. Nevertheless, there is a lot of good work that we can do now and lay positive groundwork for the future.

In nearly every organization I have worked in, the senior management team has had little or no interest in Lean. Never did that stop me from doing what I thought was right, which were these two fundamental things:

- Improve processes to benefit my internal and external customers.
- Improve myself using my own method called "continuous personal improvement."

My approach was to educate myself in Lean management and take advantage of any opportunities to participate in kaizen. This combined learning – thinking and doing – began around 1992 and has continued ever since. What I try to do is create a micro Lean environment. That means, I apply Lean principles and practices to my own work processes, and that of the people who report to me or with whom I share processes (and being very careful to assure non-zero-sum outcomes). I do this quietly and seek no recognition by my management. All I want to do is learn and improve, which itself provides all the reward I could ever ask for. Doing this makes me happy and reduces stress because I am changing, for the better, that which is under my control.

My daily practice is extremely valuable because it allows me to continuously learn about Lean management and improve my skills as a Lean leader. While I would like to do much more on a broader organizational scale, this is good for now. If opportunities to do more arise, then I will be prepared to make greater contributions because of my years of daily practice. If, in my current place of employment, no CEO ever embraces Lean, then I will still have done many good things. In addition, by eliminating waste, unevenness, and unreasonableness, I create my own internal paradise. Ahhhh…. it's so nice.

In contrast, I see many people who think it is not worth the effort to learn and practice Lean management. They have no interest in creating their own micro Lean environment. Instead, they are waiting for their CEO to "get it," at which point they will then start to apply Lean principles and practices to help create a macro Lean environment. Or, they simply won't do anything because their boss will not reward them for doing Lean.

The problem with this attitude is that you lose valuable time, ignore important opportunities to improve yourself and work processes, and will not be prepared to perform when the time comes. In the meantime, you will live with repetitive process problems that cause chronic stress and frustration, which are bad for one's health. Wouldn't you rather create a little paradise for yourself and your direct reports?

Think of this in terms of how young rock-and-roll musicians would prepare themselves to perform on stage. The bassist, for example, spends a lot of time in the basement learning how to play, in preparation for someday joining others in a band. The band then practices a lot together (and separately), in preparation to play small local venues. These small concerts give the band the live playing experience they need to play venues further from home.

That, in turn, gives them more experience and may, with some luck, lead to performing in larger venues. Never did the bassist think that the only time it would be worth committing to daily bass-playing practice was if the band secured a major gig at a prestigious venue. You have to work up to that. Practice first, then get the gig – not vice versa. People interested in Lean management should think as musicians do. First, practice (a lot), then get the gig.

Lesson 34

Managers as Queues

The method that managers normally use to process information is batch-and-queue. As a result, managers often delay taking action or making decisions. Sometimes the delays are necessary and legitimate, but most are not. Because of batch-and-queue information processing, managers can inadvertently harm efforts by people at lower levels to improve material and information to flow. While we have many Lean tools to improve the technical aspects of material and information flow, we have only education and training to help managers' desire and ability to improve flow in the work processes that they own.

The origins of the word management is "to handle," so a manager's job is to handle things. To dramatize managers' batch-and-queue information processing, imagine if we used the word "queue" ("tail," in French) instead of the word "manager." Doing so would emphasize the effect of *waiting*, which would be a better description of the problem than the *size* of the "batch." This squares with reality because we are usually far more upset with management delays than the batch size of information that managers deal with (though the two are obviously related).

Using queue as the common term for manager might help managers realize that they often make people wait in line (hence, "tail"), causing disruptions in material and information flows. In addition, managers often behave in ways that cut off the flow of information from the bottom up. These behaviors create information queues that result in the periodic surprises that managers dislike so much. If it were customary to refer to managers as queues, then we would say things like:

- "I have to schedule a meeting with my queue."
- "My queue is away on a business trip."
- "My queue wants me to think outside the box."

- "The queues want us to reduce lead-time."

Everyone would quickly realize that the job of the manager is not "to handle" things (which implies immediately, or nearly so), but instead to delay things and to make people wait. Few managers would think of themselves as queues and would likely justify delays in action or decision-making. Regardless, this is a big problem.

Why do managers delay things and make people wait? It is because managers are human, which means we are all are subject to the following:

- Faulty assumptions
- Illogical thinking
- Decision-making traps
- Overconfidence
- Mistaking beliefs for facts
- Uncertainty
- Distractions (organizational politics)
- Being inflexible
- Status quo oriented
- Making or repeating mistakes

If managers saw themselves as queues, then they might begin to think about solutions. They would start to do experiments in small PDCA problem-solving cycles and learn how to reduce and eliminate the number of queues, queue times, and batch sizes for information processing.

This is indeed what some leaders do when they re-orient themselves from command-and-control to servant leadership. Lean leaders, of course, develop awareness of the many ways they can inhibit flow through participation in kaizen. Not being status quo oriented they seek to improve themselves and their managerial capabilities in ways that are consistent with Lean principles and practices.

If you are a manager, then think of yourself as a queue (and the higher you are in the organization, the more likely you are a larger and slower-moving queue). This perspective might help motivate you to learn and improve, and become the Lean leader that so many organizations desperately need.

It's OK to evolve.

Lesson 35

Respect Employees, Respect Time

The Lean management system evolved over decades as a better way to satisfy customers in competitive, demand-driven buyers' markets. That means it recognizes the importance of time. In contrast, conventional management, which is based on batch-and-queue processing, is best suited for non-competitive, supply-driven sellers' markets. It does not recognize the importance of time. While non-competitive, supply-driven sellers' markets are fairly common, most organizations face competitive, demand-driven buyers' markets. Lean management should be the desired management system for nearly every organization. Yet, it is the practical choice which most executives ignore. Why?

Senior managers greatly prefer non-competitive, supply-driven sellers' markets and will always try to achieve this condition for some or all product lines because it makes life easier for them. They (the supplier) control price, delivery, quality, and other important terms of sale. Unfortunately, knowing how to lead a business this way will assure management complacency to customers' interests. And, senior managers will always have great difficulty learning how to compete when demand-driven buyers' markets eventually emerge for the goods and services that they provide to customers. Fundamentally, they do not understand time.

The way many organizations cope with this transition from sellers' to buyers' markets is to adopt Lean management. But most only go part of the way to Fake Lean. That means they create more efficient batch-and-queue processing, with little or no actual material and information flow. Getting material and information to flow is difficult, and most senior managers are not up to the task. They are willing to change how they think and do things, but only a little bit. They are not willing to go all the way and learn how to practice Lean management with distinction. Despite all the talk of doing things faster, reducing lead-times, delivering on-time, etc., senior managers still do not understand time if they refuse to give up batch-and-queue processing (and, relatedly, economies of scale).

The desired condition is to get material and information to flow without interruption. That means reducing batch sizes and eliminating queues. Queues, of course, are places for material and information to rest, even though they need no rest, and which increase the time it takes to complete a job or to satisfy customer demand. An organization cannot compete on the basis of time if queues are many and long in duration. Most of the technical aspects of reducing batch sizes and eliminating queues were reduced to practice and documented in the early 1900s. But the technical aspect is not all there is to it. There is a (human) behavioral aspect that greatly impacts material and information flow.

Have you ever thought about the relationship between the "Respect for People" principle in Lean management and time? Start with the opposite: what is the relationship between disrespect for people and time? Think about what happens when employees are treated in disrespectful ways by managers, such as: embarrassed in front of others; ideas shot-down; unwarranted, ill-timed, non-specific, or non-constructive criticism; interrupted in conversation; answering text messages during someone's presentation; unclear expectations; given meaningless busy work; blamed for errors, organizational politics, etc. Employees who experience these wasteful management behaviors will be demotivated, slow down, withhold information, and may look for opportunities to get even (e.g. re-order the work).

Management's bad behaviors – their disrespect for people – drive employees to process material and information related to their job using the batch-and-queue method. In addition, manager's faulty assumptions, illogical thinking, and bad decisions distract employees, which increases information batch sizes and creates larger queues as people slowly sort through things they do not understand (e.g. passive-aggressive behaviors).

It should be obvious to senior managers, but it is not, that wasteful management behaviors inhibit or block material and information flows. If senior managers behave in ways that generate waste, unevenness, and unreasonableness, then most managers below them will do the same, and the workers will respond to this by slowing things down. In addition, they will keep their ideas and creativity to themselves and will not be fully engaged in identifying and correcting problems. Employees will limit their efforts to perfunctory, check-the-box activities, to satisfy management.

The eighth waste, behavioral waste, causes the loss of human creativity and diminishes employees' desire to be curious and ask questions. It also changes the sense of time in business. When I look at a clock, I see seconds, minutes, and hours. When managers exhibit behavioral waste ("fat behaviors"), the clock immediately changes to days, weeks, and months. The disrespectful ways in which many managers treat employees (or suppliers, customers, etc.) instantly activates batch-and-queue material and information processing and makes it take a lot longer to get things done. It is no wonder that things which should take a few hours to complete end up taking weeks or months.

Unfortunately, managers do not notice the time lost by disrespecting employees. They think they can behave in ways that create waste, unevenness, and unreasonableness with zero consequences. Remarkably, their results-focused mindset misses this critically important result. Managers who have this perspective generate countless tactical and strategic problems, and then look to hire expensive superstars to fix things. They will not be able to fix anything. Managers' behavioral waste reveals self-centeredness, acceptance of chronic leadership problems, and a lack of desire to help employees (and suppliers) succeed. Behavioral waste would be my top concern if I were

CEO or served on a Board of Directors because it is the wellspring of problems.

It is an essential function of leaders to comprehend how their behaviors affect time, and do their best to behave in ways that improve material and information flow. Lean management requires senior managers to practice Lean behaviors. If not, they best they will achieve is Fake Lean. Further, it is not management's job to set employees up to fail by behaving in ways that block material and information flow, just as it is not their job to ignore processes have high failure rates – which is the guaranteed outcome of being results-focused. With the "Respect for People" principle, the clock is restored to seconds, minutes, and hours, as it should be. Now management understands time.

Respecting employees respects time, which, in turn, respects customers (and therefore investors).

REAL Lean leaders recognize the direct connection between leadership behaviors, time, and material and information flow. This is a far more practical way to understand leadership than that based on personal strengths or special characteristics such as charisma. And, importantly, it connects directly to an organization's daily business activities.

This perspective of leadership is unique, one that I originated, improved upon, and have worked to advance for over 15 years.

Lesson 36

Hordes of Hoarders

Taiichi Ohno, credited as the architect of Toyota's production system (TPS), was concerned that human nature would stand in the way of managers' ability to understand TPS and achieve flow. In his 1988 book, *Toyota Production System*, Ohno noted that people are accustomed to processing work using the batch-and-queue method (p. 10), which means they like to stockpile raw materials, work-in-process, and finished goods. He said inventories reflect a natural human behavior to hoard things in preparation for bad times, but that we should not get stuck on this way of thinking because it is no longer practical in demand-driven buyers' markets (pp. 14-15). Ohno said it would require a "revolution in consciousness" by business people to overcome their obsession for hoarding. Indeed.

While Ohno was no doubt correct, most business people do not like revolutions of any kind. Frederick Winslow Taylor said in the early 1900s that his Scientific Management system required a "mental revolution" by managers, particularly with respect to improving relationships between management and labor. Business people never liked Taylor's "mental revolution" idea. They are far more comfortable with evolution than revolution.

Since batch-and-queue thinking is so deeply embedded in the human brain, extraordinary effort must be applied to break free of this way of thinking. Normally, when we possess a physical or mental habit that we want to change, we commit ourselves to the daily practice of new routines. If we want to break free of batch-and-queue thinking, we have to learn to see batches and queues of material and information and engage in new and unfamiliar concepts and processes to reduce or eliminate them.

Obviously, this is difficult to do. After many years of effort, the best that most organizations have been able to do is process material and information in a hybrid batch-and-queue / Lean way. Flow remains elusive, which underscores Ohno's point that our basic nature is to hoard things in case trouble arises.

In recent years, attempts to achieve flow have been disrupted by senior managers who view de-coupling of processes in a value stream as a more efficient and lower cost way to process material and information. Different types of work that were at one time done in close proximity are now distributed across the globe.

Design work is done in California; engineering is done in Connecticut; manufacturing is done in China; assembly is done in Mexico; and customer service is done in India. Human nature does indeed stand in the way of understanding and achieving flow.

I experienced this first-hand when I worked in industry. I have also experienced this first-hand in the Lean leadership training that I have done since 1999. The fundamental objective of my training is to teach executives that leading organizations for flow is different, both broadly and in detail, than leading organizations for batch-and-queue (or hybrid). Senior managers' beliefs, behaviors, and competencies are completely different.

To get good at anything you have to understand the details. This is where most senior managers fall down with respect to both Lean management and Lean leadership. Here are a few of the many things that I have learned over the years doing executive training:

- If details are provided in ways that are easy to understand, some executives will say, "I already know that." But they surely do not; they think they know it because it has been presented in an easy-to-understand way. They confuse knowing with doing. They do not know or do flow.

- If details are provided in ways that are challenging to understand, some executives will say, "That's too much detail." The details, of course, are critical to Lean success. Ask any professional musician, golfer, visual artist, opera singer, etc., about the importance of details.

- If insufficient details are provided, then some executives will say, "That's too high-level. Give me more specifics." However, the specifics are what executives must learn through their own daily application of Lean principles and practices. I cannot do it for them. An old and renowned piano teacher once told his most accomplished young student, "Now you must make the piano sing." Just that; nothing more specific. For serious students, that advice is more than sufficient for them discover the next level of detail and bring joy to music lovers.

- If insufficient details are provided, then some executives will say, "That's theory." Executives misuse the word theory to describe something that they are not familiar with. Theory, of course, is an explanation for an experimentally testable hypotheses that others can replicate via experiments. I do not purvey in theory; I leave that to others.

- Even if I can absolutely, unquestionably, irrefutably, categorically, infallibly, and conclusively prove, with God in total agreement, that REAL Lean management will do great things for an organization, the top executive will often say "No thanks." They will get the business to where it needs to be by other means. They do not want to understand the details of Lean management or Lean leadership. They do not want to let go of their batch-and-queue (hoarding) mentality, etc.

Lean must be led by senior managers because it is a different way of thinking and doing things. If senior managers do not lead, then Lean will have no chance as a management system, but will instead exist ephemerally as an assortment of tools, often used incorrectly, to cut costs and improve productivity (mainly in operations).

This is what we see in most organizations. It is the popular version of Lean that over the years I have variously referred to as "Imitation Lean," "Scary Lean," and "Fake Lean" – and now, "Pop Lean" (as in pop music). This popular form of Lean is formulaic and predictable, and has lots of fizz but little substance. It is shareholder-friendly (in the short-term), but is extremely employee, supplier, and community unfriendly. Like pop music, Pop Lean (adapted from Wikipedia):

- Appeals to a general audience.
- Emphasizes craftsmanship rather than formal artistic [creative] qualities.
- Emphasizes bureaucratic conformance over spontaneous performance.
- Reflects existing trends rather than progressive developments.
- Encourages appearance over substance.

Most people like pop music, and most managers like Pop Lean. However, unlike pop music, Pop Lean can do a lot of harm. That is why Ohno (and other early pioneers of progressive management) was concerned about managers having respect for humanity, and characterized this as being of equal importance to increasing efficiency (p. xiii).

Conventional management is classical. Fake Lean is pop. REAL Lean is alternative; the alternative management genre to the hoarding status quo. Rage Against the Machine anyone? How about Tool?

Lesson 37

Can Lean Compete?

While many in the Lean community are happy with how far we have come, many are frustrated that we have not gone a lot further. If we realize that Lean management is a product that competes against other products, then maybe this will help us sharpen our focus. But we need to recognize more than just that.

Lean has many user problems. It is a complicated product compared to competing management products, which for most managers is a huge turn-off (and a big reason not to combine Lean with six sigma). In addition, there are many opportunities for users to misunderstand Lean principles, methods, and tools. I cannot tell you how many times I have seen andon lights used to blame people, Just-in-Time applied incorrectly, ordinary job tickets used as kanban cards, etc. People think the "Respect for People" principle applies only to employees, that value stream mapping itself is Lean management, that 5S is kaizen, or that any type of zero-sum (win-lose) improvement activity is kaizen. Lean might sell better if we could improve the user interface and mistake-proof it.

The persistence of these user problems indicate that most managers do not bother to do a little research to learn and understand what Lean management really is, and how to correctly apply the principles, methods, and tools. They proceed with whatever their impressions of Lean happen to be or what their peers or a consultant tells them.

One thing that all college and university professors try to do is teach students how to do research and how to think critically, because these are very important in the "real world." When students graduate and begin working, it seems most immediately forget what they learned in school about critical thinking and how to do research.

Too often, employees rely on bosses for their comprehension of Lean (and many other things), which is almost always fundamentally flawed and terribly incomplete. If, instead, graduates consistently applied critical thinking and research skills on the job, it would help them avoid a lot pain and poor outcomes caused by not understanding what they are doing.

But there is one big problem: While students are rewarded for critical thinking and doing good research, employees who think critically are often punished – especially when it comes to matters related to management and leadership (i.e. questioning the boss). They are not seen as good team members or are perceived as being difficult or as troublemakers. That happened to me on numerous occasions, as I am sure has happened to many of you. My managers and peer group were only interested in the company's flawed way of understanding and practicing Lean management (while also conforming to metrics derived from sellers' market, batch-and-queue processing). They expressed zero interest in better ways.

This is where you bump into organizational politics, a barren, lifeless desert for critical thinking. The boss-approved way of understanding and doing things is not subject to revision when new information is obtained. Instead, new information is prevented from entering into the organization. It will be allowed in when the boss says it is time to do so – perhaps several years later, or maybe never. Organizational politics assures management certitude and incuriosity, which increases risk to the enterprise and to all of its stakeholders.

Critical thinking is risky because it calls out faulty assumptions, illogical thinking, and bad decisions. Leaders who frown on critical thinking prove they do not understand Lean and are using it only to improve short-term business results. Coincidentally, those who disdain organizational politics are often the ones that do think critically and will do research to understand things better. This informs us of who is focused on doing the job well, and likely someone who is driven by intrinsic rewards. These are better candidates for advancement into leadership positions than those focused on or easily swayed by organizational politics.

Lean requires consonant leaders, those who walk the talk and do all the things necessary to learn Lean management. This is what generates people's willingness to follow their leaders and do good things. Instead, we normally experience dissonant leaders who say one thing and do another – e.g. "We want critical thinkers," then shut people down then they think critically. Lean management will not blossom under dissonant leaders and will struggle to survive in any form.

Future managers will likely associate Lean with 20th century manufacturing, high-volume work, large full-time work forces, and extensive manual labor. In a business world where computers, automation, and robots are ubiquitous, there will surely be fewer full-time employees. Many senior managers will conclude that Lean is not necessary where the types of manual work that humans do has been greatly reduced. And, in particular, people are no longer needed to drive continuous improvement; technology will do that job too (people may be so highly constrained by technology that there will be little room for process improvement). Here is the manager's equation: $T_N = I$. Meaning, new technology = improvement. This relationship will strengthen as the cost of technology for industry falls and the cycle time for new products decreases, just as it has for consumer technology, thereby making "improvement" seem continuous.

Don't ever forget that managers, throughout modern business history, have had a strong appetite for technology that displaces labor. The 1900-era standard cost accounting system told managers that labor cost is the big problem, and it is still telling them that. So, technology will continue to rule. Also, if the mindset of leadership continues to be that people are the problem, not processes, then we should expect technology to come before people. Who, then, needs the "Respect for People" principle?

Lean management offers all of us wonderful opportunities to question everything and learn new things about business, processes, and people – the kinds of things we should have learned from the start. If in the future Lean becomes widely seen by executives as more-or-less obsolete, then these opportunities will recede. It will be a century-plus missed opportunity to evolve static neo-classical economics, move away from economies of scale thinking, reform accounting systems, eliminate metrics rooted in batch-and-queue processing (planned economy, sellers' market view), and make work a more creative, interesting, and fulfilling human experience.

Here are some questions to ponder: Can Lean management compete with technology-driven business processes? Will Lean evolve in response to this? Can REAL Lean be made part of how machines think and how they process material and information? Who will do that, software developers? Will machine-made Lean created by software developers promote continuous improvement? Will RoboLean serve and respect humanity?

Lesson 38

Relatively Lean

I am very fortunate to have the best mother- and father-in-law a guy could ask for. Lou and Loretta (d. 2 May 2014) are wonderful people who have navigated life with exquisite balance and dexterity.

Loretta lived her life by many different sayings. These sayings have always struck a chord with me because they reflect various aspects of Lean thinking and doing. Here are a few examples:

- **"Eat one lasagna, make another."** A 15-pound lasagna is itself the kanban card that signals the need for replenishment.

- **"The stroonz at the top."** Leaders who shun the gemba will be viewed unfavorably.

- **"You're having another beer? How can you be so thirsty?"** Consumption should be proportional to actual need, not to what is desired.

- **"You gotta cut it up."** When you have a problem, you have to break it up into smaller pieces.

- **"You have to stick to the basics."** Getting fancy usually does not produce anything substantially better than what can be produced using the basics.

- **"Have some more."** Always be generous, never stingy. Sharing is good.

- **"Finish it."** Don't linger along and allow things to go unfinished. Get it done so you can move on to the next experiment.

- **"That's not nice."** Treat people with respect.

- **"Oh crap."** Identification of an abnormal condition.

- **"Give it a good soak."** When you start to get stale, you have to think and do something new for a while.

- **"You gotta understand."** Repetitive thinking and doing cycles (i.e. PDCA) develop one's knowledge and capabilities, which deepens one's understanding. Cannot do a good job if you don't understand.

- **"Oh, give it a shot."** Experiment and try new things.

- **"They just keep getting bigger."** Heads swell very easily. Must keep them under control.

- **"I'm going to watch you eat."** Observe to assure the planned outcome equals the expected outcome.

- **"Oh, I changed my mind."** New information should result in new direction.

Loretta knows Lean!

Lesson 39

Time to 5S Economics

As the son of a scientist, educated in engineering, and who for many years practiced the discipline, I watch the field of economics with amazement. Economists and economics are tremendously influential, whether the political party in power is right, center, or left, and can greatly influence individuals in their personal financial and non-financial decisions. In addition, our knowledge of economics, particularly ideas such as "people are rational self-interested maximizers" (i.e. selfish, zero-sum minded), can be a huge barrier to correctly understanding and practicing Lean management (see *Moving Forward Faster*, Chapter 1). Unfortunately, economics has gotten messy over time and needs some 5S.

Sort: Economics is often referred to colloquially as "the dismal science." In fact, economics is not a pure science such as mathematics or physics. It is a social science. Thinking of economics as a pure science fools people (including prominent economists) into thinking that all economic ideas are rigorous, reliable, and fact-based. The correct colloquial phrase should be "the dismal social science" or, perhaps, "the disgraceful social science" (see **Sustain**, below). Also, Adam Smith said the words "invisible hand" only once in his over 1000-page book, *The Wealth of Nations*. It was a passing comment – a way to explain what he otherwise could not explain – yet economists and others have greatly exaggerated its significance. Attributing outcomes to the "invisible hand" helps economists by freeing them from the messy job of having to systematically study causality (e.g. cheating). The "invisible hand" is repeatedly and improperly invoked as the *force majeure* of economics. It is like always saying "shit happens" when products fail or services don't deliver. Stop it.

Straighten: Economies of scale (EoS) is deeply embedded in economic thought, and therefore also deeply embedded in management thinking in both manufacturing and service organizations. It is easy to see why: just produce more and costs magically go down (and EoS is also consistent with the supply-side economics that executives favor). But there is one problem: EoS depicts amortization of cost over volume in batch-and-queue material and information processing, not flow. I have always found it unusual that economists never recognized Ford's or Toyota's flow production systems as anything more than minor tweaks to batch-and-queue processing. Flow is a huge innovation that completely upsets economies of scale (straightens out the economies of scale curve), as I pointed out in *REAL LEAN*, Volumes Five and Six. Even generations of in-house economists at General Motors and Ford have missed this. Where the heck are the Lean economists?

Shine: Economics often focuses more on the upside than on downsides (meaning, in part, that empirical results are often selectively ignored). This is driven by assumptions used in economic models to help approximate reality, but which are then forgotten when the ideas are put into practice. Thus, it can seem like benefits always greatly outweigh risks, which is then encoded into generations of management thinking. For example, economies of scale is the upside gain, while the downside risks, diseconomies of scale, are completely ignored. Another example is purchase price variance. A lower purchase price means that you have saved money. Is that so? The risks of higher costs (which usually emerge elsewhere in the business) are assumed to be small, so people do not look for them. But anyone who has taken an honest look at total costs knows that the risks, in most cases, are not small. In fact, they can be large enough to offset all of the expected savings. Our understanding of economics will be greatly improved if both upsides and downsides were viewed more critically and assessed more even-handedly by both economists and business executives.

Standardize: Each fall one or more economists win a "Nobel Prize" in economics. Unfortunately, there is no such thing as a Nobel Prize in Economics, nor a "Nobel laureate" in Economics. Alfred Nobel's will established (in 1895) prizes in Physics, Chemistry, Physiology or Medicine, Literature, and Peace, but not in Economics. A non-Nobel award for economics was established in 1968 via an association between the Royal Swedish Academy of Sciences and a Swedish bank, Sveriges Riksbank. The correct name of the Economics prize is "Sveriges Riksbank Prize in Economic [Social] Sciences in Memory of Alfred Nobel," or "SR Prize" for short. I hope that is what all SR laureates put on their lengthy resumes.

Sustain: In the old days, economics was referred to as "political economy" in acknowledgment of the close association between the state (political function) and economics. Over time, the word "political" was dropped. I think the word "political" should be re-introduced. The going-forward phrase should be "political economics," to acknowledge the reality of the close association between politics (a social clique) at state, national, and global levels, and economics (also a social clique). How else can you explain the continued existence of bad economic ideas, theories, and practices (zombie economics), which largely serve no purpose other than to prop up a favored political ideology? In science and engineering, which are largely non-political, ideas proven to be bad are quickly abandoned and never used again. Depoliticizing economics would finally allow many bad ideas to fall away and let the good ideas prosper. But since economics is a social science, it is unlikely to ever be de-politicized. It should therefore be called exactly what it is: "political economics."

Safety: I normally dislike adding additional Ss to 5S, but let's go ahead and add one more: Safety. Namely, citizens want and should demand safety in the economic system. In the past 10 years there have been two economic crises that have severely impacted people at all income levels. After 500 years of economic study, it is fair to ask the question: What has this discipline taught us about avoiding financial crises (economic instability)? When the macro-economy falters, winners of the prestigious SR Prize simply guess at what caused the problem. This is remarkable given the exalted status of economists and the stakes that are so very high. Can we afford to guess at the cause of macro-economic problems that bankrupt businesses, wipe out trillions of dollars of household wealth, and cause miserable, lingering unemployment? I want to see our SR Prize winners do formal root cause analysis and identify practical countermeasures when macroeconomic failures occur, and then demand implementation of practical countermeasures by policy makers. But we know that root cause analysis fails when the process is tainted by politics or when it is used as a tactic to assign blame. It seems we cannot have a more stable economic system until economics becomes depoliticized. For the sake of all humankind, economists, please respect people and depoliticize your discipline.

Lesson 40

Fake Lean Sells

Consultants are usually part of every organization's Lean transformation. There are some excellent consultants whose services are invaluable – especially if senior managers take advantage of their knowledge *and* get personally involved in learning Lean principles and practices. They will teach the C-level team many new and valuable ways of thinking and doing things. Others, however, will get the company started on the wrong path, as history has long shown (see my *REAL LEAN* book series, Volume Two, Chapter 3; Volume Three, Chapter 1; Volume Four, Chapter 5; Volume Six, Chapter 3). This will result in temporary improvements, usually at employees' and suppliers' expense. Executives are then faced with large amounts of re-work if they want to get Lean right, or may abandon Lean management because it failed to meet expectations.

The chances of getting started on the wrong path are great. To gain customers quickly, many consultants will supply decision-makers with lots of information that confirms their biases. If decision-makers think Lean and six sigma belong together, then so be it; together they belong! Who are they to tell executives that Lean is a management system while six sigma is a tool, one that is inconsistent with Lean because of its complexity and the need for specialists? If decision-makers think Lean is zero-sum cost-cutting, then so be it; cost-cutting it is! Who are they to tell executives that Lean is a growth strategy to achieve better outcomes for all key stakeholders?

Given how Lean management changes everything, executives who are interested in Lean should be very careful about whom they hire to help assure their Lean transformation begins well. So, allow me to offer a bit of advice on some key things to look for in Lean consultant's services – assuming senior managers want to do a good job.

- Executives should closely examine the offerings of Lean consultants to see if they present Lean as a bunch of tools (Fake Lean), or do they present Lean as a non-zero-sum principle-based management system – "Continuous Improvement" and "Respect for People" – focused on creating value for end-use customers by eliminating waste, unevenness, and unreasonableness using the Scientific Method (REAL Lean).

- How does the consultant understand and present the "Respect for People" principle? We know this principle is required for Lean transformation success, and a primary cause for failure when it is absent. Yet, this principle is usually ignored by consultants. Is the "Respect for People" principle made explicit across its many dimensions, or is it implicit (i.e. vaguely embedded in the training) and therefore easily overlooked? Is it understood only in terms of employees? Or, is it understood in terms of each key stakeholders: employees, suppliers, customers, investors, communities, and competitors? If it is just employees, then the consultant is not very good.

- Does the consultant understand the relationship between the "Continuous Improvement" and "Respect for People" principles? Can they fill out a matrix explaining the relationships between the two? If not, why not?

- Most executives, narrowly focused on profits, fail to see how the "Respect for People" principle helps improve profits. Businessman Frank Woollard has this to say about the importance of the "Respect for People" principle in 1954: "This principle… is not based on altruistic ideals – much as these are to be admired – but upon the hard facts of business efficiency." Translation: You won't get flow without it. Consultants must work harder to get this critically important point across to their customers.

- Does the consultant understand and present Lean as zero-sum (win-lose) or non-zero-sum (win win)? Does the consultant vigorously promote two win-win signature characteristics of Lean management: qualified job guarantee – no layoffs due to kaizen – and quarterly profit sharing? If not, then the consultant is, sorry to say, awful.

Fake Lean is common. Fake Lean has been around for decades. Fake Lean hurts people. Fake Lean sells. But, you don't have to buy it! Do we really want zero-sum Fake Lean to be the way that people think of Lean management? Or, do we want to improve? In my view, consultants, in general, must be more aggressive at promoting REAL Lean. In addition, organizations can achieve greater Lean success by more carefully specifying and evaluating the services offered by consultants.

Still, consultants can take an organization only so far. Greater success will be realized if every member of the C-level team commits to learning Lean management through personal engagement in kaizens, etc.

I am a teacher, not a consultant. I write to inform and educate. The more you know, the better able you will be to write your request for proposal and evaluate consultant's responses (while you are at it, ask for disclosure of downside risks and timing). My work will help both consultants and their customers get off to a better start.

People's lives depend on it.

Lesson 41

Ten Whys? Why Not?

Lean practitioners are no doubt familiar with "5 Whys" method of root cause analysis. For over a decade I have required my students to do root cause analysis using the 5 Whys method in most of the undergraduate and graduate courses that I teach. I do this because I think it is important for them to understand and practice the method, and then apply it on-the-job.

Every semester, I tell my students: "5 Whys is the name of the method, but do not stop your analysis at the fifth why. Keep going until you arrive at the root cause." But what do you think happens most of the time? Students stop at the 5th why, even though their analysis is obviously incomplete.

Unfortunately, the name "5 Whys" anchors students so strongly that most do not continue their analysis to why number 6, why number 7, and so on, if their analysis warrants it. In most cases it does. Beginning in the fall 2010 semester, we no longer used the "5 Whys." Instead, we began using the "10 Whys," and something remarkable happened: students began doing more complete analyses, and most arrived at actual root causes. Perhaps your organization would also benefit by using the "10 Whys" instead of the 5 Whys.

While students' root cause analyses have greatly improved, I am often dissatisfied with the countermeasures that they identify. Their countermeasures tend to be impractical or simply state what someone should do better. The countermeasures must have much greater process focus and also be consistent with the "Respect for People" principle.

Speaking of "Respect for People," every semester I ask my graduate students, most of whom have 10 or more years of professional work experience, a simple question: "Have you ever seen an executive, vice president-level or above, show you their root cause analysis of one of their management problems?" The answer, 100 percent of the time, has been "No," from thousands of students over the last 13 years.

This is remarkable because almost every senior manager in the organizations my students come from – manufacturing, service, non-profit, and government organizations – have been trained in problem-solving processes, including root cause analysis. In some cases, root cause analysis is a deeply embedded part of the company's operating system. But not for senior managers, it seems.

Apparently most executives do not think root cause analysis (or A3 reports) applies to their job or to management problems. They are under the illusion that root cause analysis is only for technical problems and not useful for problems in human resource, sales, finance, purchasing, etc. This view, fortunately, seems to be slowly changing in some industries.

Part of being an effective Lean leader means to be consistent in words and actions. If management expects workers to use problem-solving processes for the problems they encounter, then managers at all levels should be doing the same. Executives must show employees objective evidence of their use of root cause analysis and the identification and implementation of practical countermeasures. If senior managers do that often, then employees will follow their lead.

Next, I have to start asking my students if they have ever seen any visual controls in executives' offices for the leadership processes that they participate in. I do not mean performance metrics dashboards. I mean the executive equivalent of shop- and office-floor visual controls for daily management of the 15 or so fundamental processes that executives participate in. Do they use standardized work and checklists? Are the top five management errors posted for all to see? What do decision-making quality problems look like? This is what anyone in a position of responsibility should do to help eliminate errors and re-work. How do you think my students will respond?

Lesson 42

Flow is Fundamentally Different

People who have the kinds of jobs that require daily practice, such as athletes or musicians, freely acknowledge that they are never done learning. They accept that they must practice the fundamentals, as well as more advanced techniques, for decades. It would be unusual to hear a musician say: "I'm beyond that" or "I already know that" – the implication being that the musician has a complete understanding of some particular aspect of music.

When it comes to Lean management, in whole or part, most managers are very quick to say: "I'm beyond that" or "I already know that" – the implication being that the manager has a complete understanding of management. I have heard this countless times by managers in reference to Lean. Some managers say "I'm beyond that" or "I already know that" simply as an excuse to avoid Lean. That is probably better than saying "I'm beyond that" or "I already know that" and actually thinking they really do know that.

Managers often claim knowledge and skill levels with respect to Lean that they cannot possibly possess because they do not even practice the fundamentals. This is obvious, simply by speaking to them, as they cite various recurring business problems and other abnormal conditions that diligent practice of Lean would have greatly reduced or eliminated.

The phenomenon that superficial knowledge of Lean management can substitute for the skills developed by daily practice is probably is tied, in part, to corporate hierarchies, in which people in superior positions assume themselves to be smarter the those in subordinate positions. The bigger the title or higher the grade level, the more likely a small amount of knowledge will be mistaken for deep levels of knowledge, skill, or capability.

In addition, successful people often have experienced decades of positive feedback, starting with good grades in school to rapid advancement at work. That can make anyone feel as if they know more than they actually do. I have a saying, congruent with Lean thinking, to address this attitude. It is:

"Don't confuse getting an 'A' or receiving
a diploma with knowing anything."

This saying can be controversial among executives from countries where diplomas are highly regarded as proof of knowledge and competency. Face the facts: They learned, explicitly or implicitly, batch-and-queue material and information processing. They do not learn flow, except in rare cases. Good grades and diplomas should not leave anyone with an impression that they know anything about Lean management. Technical diplomas are yesterday's news. They are OK, "as far as that goes."

Batch-and-queue processing and flow are two vastly different knowledge areas. The point of saying, "Don't confuse getting an 'A' or receiving a diploma with knowing anything," is to remind senior managers leaders that they must always think, apply Lean principles and practices daily, and ask why in non-blaming, non-judgmental ways.

Flow is unlike anything anyone has been taught in school. I have never heard a capable Lean leader say: "I'm beyond that" or "I already know that." They are humble because they know there is much more to learn about business and management, and they remain committed to daily practice of the fundamentals. They are dedicated readers, both as a means to keep thinking and as a source for new ideas to experiment with on-the-job.

Lesson 43

Two Definitions to Know

Surprisingly, Lean management existed without rigorous definition for decades. Some see merit in that because having no definition requires people to think for themselves. Presumably, their definition of Lean will evolve over time and become a more accurate representation of what Lean management really is. While that may happen in some cases, the unfortunate reality, however, is that most people do not think for themselves. Therefore, they will quickly define Lean in whatever ways they like or they will adopt definitions – often very bad ones – that they have heard from others. Leaders of organizations who do this (and most do) transfer mistaken views of Lean to followers. Then, people like me have to expend great energy to correct these widespread, mistaken views of Lean. It is an unnecessary rework loop.

Undefined, Lean becomes anything and everything, and thus loses its meaning. Over time, this leads to widespread confusion and profound misunderstandings and misapplications of Lean management. Variation in people's definition reduces the meaning and significance of Lean over time and has led to big problems such as the pervasiveness Fake Lean, incorrect use of tools and methods, bureaucratization of Lean in large organizations, and so on.

Here is a definition of Lean management that I have used for many years:

> A non-zero-sum principle-based management system focused on creating value for end-use customers and eliminating waste, unevenness, and unreasonableness using the Scientific Method.

Cumbersome? Yes it is. But the definition is accurate. Importantly, I have found that this definition helps leaders to begin to think for themselves because they are unfamiliar with every component of this definition. They are unfamiliar with non-zero-sum (win-win), principles, value, end-use customers, waste, unevenness, unreasonableness, and the Scientific Method. In the conventional management practice that most executives know, each of these elements are missing because they are not considered important to the function of business.

My definition gets people thinking and helps drive home the point that Lean management is vastly different than the conventional management they have long known. It also has profound implications for Lean leadership.

As a Lean practitioner, you will learn, sooner or later, what all Lean practitioners learn: it is not Lean tools alone that deliver success. The critical element is leadership.

What does "leadership" mean? There are hundreds of definitions of leadership, nearly all of which are abstract and focus on the leader. For Lean management, the definition of leadership must be practical and focus on followers. The definition of Lean leadership that I have used for many years is:

> Beliefs, behaviors, and competencies that demonstrate respect for people, motivate people, improve business conditions, minimize or eliminate organizational politics, ensure effective utilization of resources, and eliminate confusion and rework.

No definition is perfect, and nearly every word in any definition requires further definition. However, this definition accurately reflects what Lean management requires of its leaders, and it is more specific and actionable. Importantly, it helps get material and information to flow.

Fundamentally, what "leadership" means is that aspiring Lean leaders will have to learn many new things, both technical and behavioral. And, they will also need to learn the nuances and details of Lean management in order to skillfully lead a Lean transformation.

One very important thing that senior managers will have to learn is the relationship between the "Continuous Improvement" and "Respect for People" principles. Few people ever consider this because most focus on only the "Continuous Improvement" principle, and because these relationships are not obvious. This truly is the core of Lean management; something that leaders must know.

Lesson 44

Combining Values

Many people have a deep dislike for progressivism, in general, and for one of its offshoots, progressive management, beginning with Frederick Winslow Taylor's Scientific Management (from which Lean has evolved). Why? Progressivism has been roundly criticized for 100 years because it is seen as possessing negative attributes such as the cult of expertise, faith in science for social reform, perfecting people by perfecting society, etc. Progressive haters work very hard to limit or derail progressivism wherever it appears. Could this be why REAL Lean is so hard to find, while Fake Lean is pervasive?

Unfortunately, stereotypes and knee-jerk reactions cut off inquiry, which, if made, would reveal that the progressive management of 2015, like the progressive management of 1915, has always been a unique combination of the best of both conservative and liberal values – what I called "conserberal" in Chapter 5 of *REAL LEAN: The Keys to Sustaining Lean Management* (Volume Three). Unfortunately, nuance is not easy to discuss with those who have a strong dislike of progressivism and dismiss ideological amalgamations, even thoughtful ones.

People who want to limit or derail progressivism wherever it appears will typically use a core strategy of ignoring rules for argumentation and ignoring facts. (I recommend reading the little book, *Being Logical: A Guide to Good Thinking*, by D.Q. McInerny, to gain a more comprehensive understanding of the illogical arguments used). This strategy, as well as the specific tactics used, has been very effective in derailing progressive management principles and practices.

Lean people should become familiar with the strategy and tactics because that is what they confront every day with skeptical managers and others. Put another way, if we want to advance

Lean, we must thoroughly understand the strategy and tactics that people have long used to limit or derail our well-intentioned progressive efforts to eliminate waste, unevenness, and unreasonableness, and to do so in non-zero-sum (win-win) ways.

In addition, we must do a far better job of convincing business leaders of the merits of Lean management, most of whom dislike progressivism in almost any form. The overarching selling point has to be that Lean management is an effective combination of conservative and liberal values rooted in profit-seeking capitalism, from the beginning, and driven by mutual respect to achieve shared prosperity.

It must become seen as a significant improvement over conventional management. The sooner the better, for all.

Lesson 45

The Middle Manager Problem

It is common to hear senior managers say that the company's Lean transformation efforts were slowed due to resistance from middle managers. They usually attribute the resistance to Lean or a fear of change. Senior managers have perceived a problem (an effect) and identified two causes. Unfortunately, they have not identified the real problem and are guessing at the causes, which will surely lead to guessing solutions such as: "We don't have the right people in these key positions" or "We need new managers." These will not correct the problem.

If we look at this problem from middle managers' perspective, we would see more than just two causes that contribute to the problem perceived by senior managers. Middle managers would say:

- I don't understand Lean management.
- I don't know what to do.
- My boss does not support Lean.
- My boss does not practice Lean.
- Lean is for operations people; I'm not in operations.
- There are no rewards or recognition for doing Lean.
- Lean is just another demand placed upon me. It's a burden.
- There is nothing in it for me.
- I am afraid of losing my job.
- I fix things; continuous improvement is continuous re-work.
- I don't like rapid change.
- I am worried about failing and the consequences.
- Top management wants "flawless execution" and says "failure is not an option."

- I fear being blamed for bad outcomes.
- My job description has not changed.
- I don't have time for Lean.
- I keep forgetting what to do.
- My boss holds me accountable for results.
- My peers are not doing Lean and they still get rewarded.
- Annual performance appraisal criteria have not changed.
- Promotion criteria have not changed.
- I am held accountable to the same old metrics.

There is much more going on here than just resistance or fear of change. Lean transformations that go too slowly suffer from structural problems, not from a middle manager problem.

It is clear that the problem is an absence of problem-solving by senior managers. They must clarify the perceived problem because it is different from the actual problem(s). The actual problem correlates better with senior managers not having done the work necessary to set middle managers up to succeed.

Senior managers need to do an A3 report for this problem to understand root causes, and also to eliminate blame. If they did so, they would find numerous causes for the narrow effect that they perceive, and nearly every cause they find would require a corrective action – all of which would be relatively simple. Three things stand out with respect to slow Lean transformations:

- Senior management inconsistency.
- Lack of specificity regarding new roles, responsibilities, and daily activities.
- Poor understanding of Lean principles and practices by senior managers, which impedes their ability to explain and teach Lean management to middle managers.

In most Lean transformations, senior managers do not do the things they expect middle managers to do. Senior managers support Lean, but they do not act as role models by applying

Lean principles and practices to their own work and other work activities (by participating in kaizen). To say Lean is important and then personally do nothing says it all: "Lean is for lower-level people to do, not me." It also says that Lean management is not that important. Senior managers willingly throw away a great opportunity to lead by example. This is an obvious leadership problem that must be corrected.

Senior managers must be explicit regarding what middle managers should do differently day-to-day. That means, in part, addenda to all job descriptions that include (as a starting point):

- Eliminate waste, unevenness, and unreasonableness.
- Use structured problem-solving tools (i.e. A3 and A4 reports).
- Create visual controls.
- Improve flow, then improve it again and again.
- Respect people: employees, suppliers, customer, investors, and communities.

Of course, senior managers must do these same things in their own work activities if they expect middle managers to do them in theirs. The expectation should be established that middle managers will describe these new activities at least weekly at the gemba (not in a conference room), and that senior managers will show evidence of their efforts to solve problems and improve processes to all employees (seeing, after all, is believing). Expectations, of course, must be followed up with concrete actions.

Senior managers must also be able to explain how Lean management makes middle manager's job better and easier. If middle managers perceive Lean to make their job more difficult or worse, then one cannot expect them to embrace Lean management. Senior managers frequently pile requirements onto middle managers with no indication of what activities can be eliminated. This leaves middle managers to decide what is important and what is not important. In most cases, middle managers will continue to do only what they are used to doing – especially if anti-Lean metrics remain in place.

What I have tried to illustrate here is that senior managers have a lot of work to do. They cannot simply proclaim the adoption of Lean management and then walk away from it or pretend to be interested during monthly reviews. Senior managers have to be part of it. They have to recognize that non-zero-sum (win-win) Lean is not a minor change to what they already know about people, work, organization, management, and leadership. It's back to school. If that is too big a challenge for them, then they should not adopt Lean management or find a different job.

Lesson 46

Do Not Distract the Value-Adders

Distracted driving has become a topic of considerable importance recently. Smart phones, texting, GPS devices, and eating fast food or drinking coffee while driving have been cited as causes of serious traffic accidents and injuries. It is sensible to be concerned about distracted driving and take appropriate action to reduce harm to self and others.

Similarly, I think we must also be concerned about distracted managing.

The effect of distracted managing is distracted work among the people who add value to the products and services that we purchase: employees and suppliers. Executives and managers should ask themselves: "Do we want distracted workers and suppliers? What harm might come of that?" It should be obvious that distracted employees and suppliers will be less likely to identify and act upon cost reduction opportunities, less likely to identify and act upon lead-time reduction opportunities, and less likely to identify and act upon quality problems in a timely manner.

What constitutes distractions in the workplace that negatively impacts employees? Here are a few to consider: revolving door management; batch-and-queue metrics; organizational politics; constant threat of layoffs, outsourcing, or offshoring - no matter how well people perform; perfunctory or politicized performance appraisals; unattainable goals; blaming people for errors; firefighting; lack of wage growth; unfair pay and benefits; not getting credit where credit is due; waste-of-time meetings; stalled decision-making; zero-sum minded management. Need I go on?

What about suppliers? Here are a few to consider: revolving door purchasing managers; batch-and-queue metrics (i.e. purchase price variance); repetitive quoting; constant threat of taking away the work; unattainable cost reduction goals, blaming suppliers for errors (when the root cause often points back to buyers); unstable schedule; firefighting; late product or service specs; cost reduction ideas that are ignored; stalled decision-making; zero-sum minded management. You get the idea.

Why would any senior executive want employees or suppliers – the value-adders – to de distracted? It can only increase costs, both financial and non-financial, and ruin your ability to compete on the basis of time.

Unfortunately, most executives probably do not think of these things as distractions. Nor do they see these distractions as abnormal conditions. Instead, they see these distractions as "part of doing business," or as "just the way things are." Obviously, such managers are incurious and have not developed their observation and thinking skills.

Lean leaders who develop observation and thinking skills soon recognize such distractions as abnormal conditions. They will then take the next steps to identify the root causes of these distractions and identify practical countermeasures. Help your value-adders – employees and suppliers – by eliminating their distractions. Have some fun and create a visual control that reminds leaders not to distract the value-adders.

Lesson 47

Disrupting Material and Information Flow

Let's explore some real-world ways in which ignorance of the "Respect for People" principle affects material and information flow, and time – especially information flow and time. This, of course, is highly relevant to the countless organizations that practice Fake Lean as well as those that strive towards REAL Lean.

Fundamentally, business is teamwork because it requires the willing participation of at least five key stakeholders: employees, suppliers, customers, investors, and communities. These human stakeholders will become unhappy whenever their interests are not respected. Acute instances of disrespect are part of business life that one must contend with. If the senior managers of an organization are mostly zero-sum (win-lose) in their thinking and actions, then the five key stakeholders will be chronically marginalized. And that is the problem. Teamwork will falter and the time it takes to get things done will increase. Information processing will be driven in the wrong direction, towards batch-and-queue – bigger batches, longer queues.

While all five key stakeholders are important (as well as competitors), let's focus on the stakeholders involved in value-creating activities: employees and suppliers. Let's look at some ways they are treated and determine if this improves information flow, or if it drives information towards batch-and-queue processing.

<u>Employees</u>

1. A boss tells an employee or small team: "Find the answer to this problem," or "Go figure out the best way to do it." That kind of direction suggests to people that they must undertake a thorough analysis, which will of course take time – typically, weeks or months. They will want to impress the boss and will

therefore thoroughly study the problem. They will report their findings as the boss's schedule permits. The direction given by the boss to "Find the answer to this problem" necessitates batch-and-queue information processing, during which time the problem lingers uncorrected. Had the manager instead said: "Find a better way," then the analysis would be quicker and improvement would be made sooner. The problem might not be "solved" in the technical sense, but the frequency and duration of the problem has been diminished through the first of many cycles of continuous improvement. Good work has been done quickly, as opposed to work that appears perfect (but isn't) that is done very slowly.

2. A young, energetic new employee is in her first meeting. The boss asks everyone for ideas – any ideas – to deal with a particular problem. She blurts out a crazy idea, immediately after which the boss leads a chorus of laughter. The new employee has been publicly humiliated. How long will it be before she employee offers another crazy idea? A week? One month? One year? Ten years? Thirty years? Never? Maybe never. Information that the company needs to improve and grow will be withheld, possibly for decades, because of this one humiliating event. The flow of crazy ideas from that person – ideas that are necessary for economic growth – have been halted. In general, one can expect the number of ideas under such circumstances to diminish, the result of managers behaving in ways that create batch-and-queue information processing.

3. A manager does what he knows he is supposed to do: ask for feedback from his team. Then, the manager does what he is not supposed to do: ignore the feedback. The team members soon realize that the manger is not actually interested in their feedback. The feedback diminishes and eventually stops. Occasionally, team members offer some feedback just to test the manager. Information processing – feedback – is now batch-and-queue.

4. A manager tells employees, "Do as you are told." They dutifully follow these instructions and do exactly as they are told. Naturally, small problems arise, but they do not tell their manager. The small problems accumulate over time until one day they become a big problem that suddenly explodes. The manager gets what he despises: a big surprise. By cutting off the flow of information, the manager has created batch-and-queue information processing that guarantees periodic ugly surprises.

5. A manager blames people for errors and is generally abusive and bullying. He is condescending and autocratic, intimidating, hypocritical, has a big ego, plays favorites, can't admit errors, and takes credit for the work of others. He is inconsistent, often saying one thing and doing another. Team members do not understand what is expected of them, and they are often confused about what they are supposed to do. What is important changes almost daily, and he is results-focused. He is deeply zero-sum (win-lose) minded and always serves self before others. However, he does a great job managing upward and navigating office politics, leading his boss to think he is a highly capable manager. Will information flow between the manager and team members? Or, between the manager and his boss? Impossible; it will surely be batch-and-queue. This is a highly incapable manager; one who must improve – quickly.

<u>Suppliers</u>

1. The finance vice president of CashCo has a brilliant idea: extend payment terms to suppliers from 30 days to 90 days to improve cash flow. The company and its investors benefit at suppliers' expense. The suppliers are displeased. They do business with hundreds of other customers whose payment terms are 30 days and are easier to work with. Soon after implementing the new payment terms, CashCo gets into a jam and suffers major delivery problems. It needs its suppliers to help get itself get out of the jam. Will suppliers be quick to help out? Some will, others will not.

2. The finance vice president of CashCo has another brilliant idea: transfer its costs to suppliers by demanding that they carry one month of inventory as part of contract terms and conditions. Suppliers have no choice but to comply. They are upset about their added cost burden and look for opportunities to even the score. Thankfully for suppliers, CashCo's engineers do a lousy job designing parts, so there are frequent engineering changes that require new tooling. So, they submit new tooling charges often. It is always a large round number, unlike the part price which is always exact to the penny. Usually, existing tooling is re-worked at a fraction of the quoted price. CashCo never checks up on this. Tooling charges, it turns out, are the supplier's profit improvement plan. They even budget for this profit in their annual financial plan because CashCo never improves its design process. It is money in the bank. By the way, suppliers don't actually carry one month of inventory. They just tell CashCo they do; CashCo never checks on that either. Zero-sum optimizations such as these, done by both buyer and seller, fracture teamwork and obstruct information flow.

3. The finance vice president of CashCo has yet another brilliant idea: throttle the production schedule to receive materials when it is financially advantageous for CashCo and defer receipt when it is not. In particular, refuse to accept deliveries from suppliers the last two days of every month and the last week of each quarter. Suppliers are furious because their financial plans are disrupted, and, on many occasions, the new production schedule pushes the finished goods out by months and pulls in other goods that have not even been started for immediate delivery. The disruption to suppliers' business is enormous and their complaints to senior managers about this problem are ignored. Suppliers focus attention and resources on their better customers.

4. The finance vice president of CashCo has still more brilliant ideas: Slow-selling products will be discounted after specific increments of time, with 100 percent of the discount funded by unilateral supplier price reduction. Say an item with a retail price

of $100, purchased from the supplier for $50, does not sell after one month. Mark the item down to $80 and automatically debit the supplier's account by $20. That helps assure CashCo's margins at the supplier's expense. Suppliers go nuts and slow down or halt shipments. They also tip off federal government investigators, eventually costing CashCo millions of dollars in legal fees. Relations with suppliers remain strained for years to come due to broken trust.

5. The finance vice president of CashCo, desperate to improve margins by cutting the prices of purchased goods and services, ignores suppliers' cost reduction suggestions. It turns out there is no budget for implementing suppliers' cost reduction suggestions, and there never will be. Instead, the finance VP sees it as more cost-effective to demand price reductions from suppliers rather than working together with them to reduce costs. Suppliers soon become frustrated and withhold future cost reduction suggestions. They also withhold suggestions for improving products, since pressure by CashCo to reduce purchase prices will only hurt them in the long run. The flow of ideas to both grow sales and cut costs has been severed by short-term zero-sum thinking. CashCo earns a new nickname among its suppliers: ScrewCo.

Of course, it does not end here. Zero-sum conventional management, by its very nature, must take advantage of every key stakeholder, in-turn or simultaneously. Customers who do not get what they want will think twice before making their next purchase. Management's desire to improve the company's position at the expense of customers introduces a delay in customer's decision-making process and hands new opportunities to competitors. The same goes for investors. Like any other stakeholder, communities are also seen as instruments to bargain with and gain advantage.

These real-world examples illustrate the effect that leadership behaviors and decisions can have on information flows. By not understanding the "Respect for People" principle, senior managers have constricted or choked-off information flows, which, in turn, diminishes teamwork and reduces employees' and suppliers' responsiveness to changing circumstances.

Senior managers should always have as their objective to think, behave, and make decisions in ways that improve (material and) information flows. That should be the normal condition. They should remove impediments to information flows, not create impediment after impediment. They should speed up material and information flows, while at the same time being very careful not to speed people up. This will improve system responsiveness, teamwork, competitiveness, and financial and non-financial performance. I am quite sure that is what senior managers want.

Lesson 48

Leading Under the Influence

Influential people and influential publications often say things that are illogical. It can go a step further in the wrong direction when illogical statements are presented as axiomatic, meaning, something that is true under all conditions. One hopes that the people and organizations that influence others would not only have their facts straight, but that they also closely examine what they say to ensure it is logical.

The problem, of course, is that influential people who do not get their facts straight or make illogical statements influence other people. The influenced simply assume that the person or organization in the superior position knows that they are talking about. Unfortunately, people in influential positions are usually no better than anyone else at getting their facts straight or assuring that their statements are logical. One's position in a hierarchy does not assure logic or accuracy. In many cases, it assures inaccuracy and illogic due to organizational or political factors such as having to agree with boss or to support a preferred ideology.

As an educator, this troubles me greatly because it speaks poorly of higher education – both undergraduate and graduate education processes (all disciplines). It also speaks poorly of promotion processes where people who do not know what they are talking about can easily advance. In addition, illogical statements are almost immediately incorporated into the thinking and speaking of other influential people, as well as people with virtually no influence. Regular employees with little influence are often solidly in agreement with management's illogical statements.

Here are some examples (names withheld to avoid blaming people) of what top managers say or think:

"My job is to maximize shareholder value."

From a mathematical perspective, shareholder value can never actually be maximized by executives because corporate debt is always much greater than zero. Executives who increase financial risk by incurring greater debt make it more difficult to maximize shareholder value. They can, however, increase stock price by reducing other costs – usually done in a zero-sum manner (see "Fair Business is Moral Business").

The CEO of a Fortune 10 conglomerate said in an e-mail to all employees:

"We all know the truth of 'what gets measured gets managed'."

The statement, "what gets measured gets managed," can be disproved in an instant using mathematical logic.

The Chief Financial Officer of a Fortune 50 conglomerate said this about management's manufacturing cost reduction strategy at an investor's conference:

"Anyplace outside of Connecticut is low-cost."

So, California is lower cost than Connecticut? New York City lower cost than Connecticut? London, Stockholm? Antarctica? The Moon? In some cases, the statement is so baldly illogical that it need not be formally tested. It is obvious upon inspection.

A variant of this phrase was later offered by a division president:

"…outside of Connecticut…
by definition is low-cost sourcing."

By definition? No. By illogical definition? Yes. These statements do not reflect fact. Instead, they reflect a specific agenda and certain desired outcomes.

An editorial in *The Economist* stated:

"Rules [regulation] raise costs by compelling businesses to do things differently."

As Lean people, one thing we know for sure is this: it is not axiomatic that changing the way you do things raises costs. When you change processes, they can be improved to yield lower costs, higher quality, shorter lead-times, etc. Process changes can raise costs by adding more steps, such as over-inspections, as is typically done in conventional management. The *Economist* editorial went on to say:

"That [regulation] is acceptable if the benefits... justify the costs."

This perspective requires someone to prove that benefits justify the costs in order for a regulation to be considered acceptable.

Therefore, if one cannot prove it, then the regulation has no merit. This is illogical because an absence of proof favoring a regulation does not provide an argument against the regulation. Also, the inability to prove that the benefits justify the costs does not disprove a regulation has merit (especially in relation to externalized costs).

Complaining about government regulation is a red herring and reflects a decline in corporate leadership thinking capabilities. Leaders should instead challenge themselves to see government regulation as a new sales opportunity or an opportunity to offer customers a better value proposition (possibly at a higher price). The topic of regulation, like politics, is a magnet for other illogical arguments such as: special pleading, false dilemma, using and abusing tradition, avoiding the force of reason, making false assumptions, and abuse of expertise.

An essay in *The Wall Street Journal* said:

"...the real problem with regulation is that it often does not work very well, in part because it's always considering problems in the rear-view mirror."

This statement reflects the businessman's view: regulation is undesirable because the next problem will be different. So, despite people being hurt by a problem, it is not necessary to investigate the problem to avoid its recurrence. In contrast, a scientist's or engineer's view would be that a problem or failure must be investigated to eliminate its recurrence. If other problems occur, same or different, then these will be investigated as well and corrective actions will be taken to eliminate their recurrence.

If regulation is not desirable due to unknown future consequences, then we have almost nothing to learn from managerial, financial, process, product, service, or any other type of failure. Instead, just move on. Mistake-making is OK, but mistake-proofing, for example, is obviously a waste of time and effort. In reality, the rear-view mirror is an integral part of improving processes. Ignore it and you ignore feedback and opportunities to improve. In conventional management, that is OK. In Lean management, it is not OK.

Unfortunately, illogical statements are rarely called out by reporters, editorial writers, investment analysts, managers, politicians, business school professors, employees, etc., which greatly handicaps our ability to learn and improve. This is one reason why Lean management emphasizes facts and logic (i.e. the Scientific Method) – which, this alone, is a colossal difference compared to conventional management.

Here is another statement for you to consider. The following was stated by a politician in support of the two-tier wage system now common in union labor contracts in the United States:

"You must have a globally competitive wage to create jobs."

Is this statement logical or illogical?

Finally, nearly every employer says they the thing they want most is to hire people with good critical thinking skills. The irony, of course, is that the examples given above show a stunning absence of critical thinking among well-educated people in influential positions.

You could say that these examples are the proof that companies do indeed need to hire people with good critical thinking skills, since it is obviously so lacking. But, what will happen to employees who call out their CEOs, CFOs, or manager's lack of critical thinking?

Alternatively, you could say that most companies *say* they want to hire people with good critical thinking skills, but that they do not actually mean it. After all, what manager wants to be put into uncomfortable positions every day?

Leading under the influence of untested beliefs and assumption and illogical thinking surely leads to poor decision-making, just as driving under the influence of drugs or alcohol does. Leaders have to be more responsible to lead effectively.

Lesson 49

Barriers to The Toyota Way

In a recent issue of *Manufacturing Engineering*, Jeffrey Liker and James Franz authored an interesting and informative article titled, "The Toyota Way: Helping Others Help Themselves." In it, they identify four main barriers to achieving the Toyota Way:

- An epidemic of short-term thinking.
- Underlying view that sees organizations as machines.
- Fundamental misunderstanding of what it takes to learn and improve.
- Misunderstanding the purpose of Lean tools.

I agree that these are barriers. However, the actual situation is far more complicated than these four main barriers suggest. Organizations' inability to achieve the Toyota Way is an effect that we have long struggled with, and have had limited success identifying causes. The question remains, why?

I too have had a close look at this problem, and my analysis, presented in my book, *Moving Forward Faster: The Mental Evolution from Fake Lean to REAL Lean*, yields a different taxonomy for the four main barriers to the Toyota Way:

- Economic
- Social
- Political
- Historical

Importantly, the economic, social, and political categories are supported by the late 1800s and early 1900s pioneers of progressive Scientific Management, the forerunner of Lean, whose work pre-dates Toyota and the Toyota Way (see *REAL LEAN*, Volume Two). This taxonomy emerges in the late

1920s, about 30 years after the birth of Scientific Management, as one way to explain the lack of penetration of this new type of progressive management in American industry. They too were amazed and frustrated that few business leaders sought to incorporate the management system in its entirety and were instead quite happy to cherry-pick some tools and settle for short-term improvements to the bottom line.

However, the pioneers failed to identify the specific elements that constitute economic, social, and political factors that impeded manager's abilities to comprehend and practice progressive management. They thought it was a problem of leadership (a subset of social psychology), a field of study that was just beginning to emerge in the early 1930s. They bet the success of their movement on social psychologists who, in time, would surely figure out the answer to their problem. They were wrong.

My contribution to the pioneers' taxonomy was to add the historical category, because we now have a much better understanding of the historical failure modes in progressive management. In addition, I identified 85 specific sub-causes for the four categories – even just a couple of which can derail an organization's efforts to achieve the Toyota Way. My analysis indicates we have a far more difficult challenge than to find practical countermeasures for the four main barriers identified by Liker and Franz.

In *Moving Forward Faster*, I identify 24 economic ways of thinking that must diminish or be eliminated; 22 social ways of thinking that must diminish or be eliminated; 18 political ways of thinking that must diminish or be eliminated; and 21 historical problems or errors that derail efforts to achieve the Toyota Way. A lot has to change; much more than we realize.

It makes intuitive sense that many more causes would contribute to the observed effect because Lean is a management system in which economic, social, and political ways of thinking about business are interconnected. In addition, The Toyota Way 2001 document itself broadly describes what has worked in the past (and thus what has not), thereby informing of readers of important historical causes which, if ignored, will make it very difficult to understand and achieve the Toyota Way.

In addition, The Toyota Way 2001 document specifically calls out the importance of the "Respect for People" principle not because it is nice to do, but because it is a business necessity. The "Respect for People" principle is how you know about problems, versus problems kept hidden because people fear being blamed. One cannot improve of one does not know about problems. Ex post facto characterization of the purpose of flow (and related Lean tools and methods) to surface problems does not square with the historical development of material and information flow in organizations in which mangers sought to improve both labor relations and basic business metrics.

Liker and Franz give us the answer to our problem: "See Lean as a system linking business strategy to personal accountability." See Lean as a system. Is this the answer? I think it is more likely that there is no answer, and that we should be prepared to accept that. As a teacher, I believe that education offers hope only to those who want to think and learn – some of it in the classroom but most of it on-the-job. The best chance to succeed will be those who rise to the challenge and practice every day.

What we have clearly learned, after decades of effort, is that the curricula for teaching Lean management to leaders should never be initially centered on tools and methods. It should instead focus on the specific ways in which Lean management challenges leaders' economic, social, and political views of business, and how to take advantage of what history has taught us. Only after that should the tools and methods be taught and put into practice by leaders.

Supplemental Note to Lesson 49

In June of 2001, I visited Toyota's Motomachi plant and asked the General Manager of final assembly, Mr. Kuzuhara, the following question: "What is the mechanism or process for maintaining discipline to 'The Toyota Way'?" He replied:

> "There was nothing on paper. It was just passed on to employees generation after generation by on-the-job-training. In 2001 Toyota published a book on The Toyota Way [in April 2001]. The book is OK, but practice by us makes the words come alive. Words are just words; there is more to it than words. For the past 50 to 60 years we have never forgotten the importance of education and training. Employees are given specific education targets in keeping with company goals. Not just desk education, but practical skills development."

The value of "The Toyota Way 2001" document to people outside of Toyota is to reinforce a fact long known by those who have succeeded in their practice of progressive management. That is, both principles, "Continuous Improvement" and "Respect for People" are required in order to achieve flow. Leaders have to put both principles into practice.

The mistake that so many people have made in the past, and still today, is that they will be able to achieve flow using only continuous improvement.

Lesson 50

The Human Case for Lean

Over the decades, many people have tried to make the business case for Lean in an attempt to gain senior management support. They typically start with arguments based on removing waste or improving efficiency. That, surprisingly, proved to be unconvincing to most executives. So, they moved on to other arguments such as improving productivity or operational excellence. Once again, that proved to be unconvincing to most executives. Then, they finally began to speak in the language of senior managers: money – specifically, increasing profit. Surprisingly, even that has been largely unconvincing, as I too learned soon after wring the book *Better Thinking, Better Results*. We wrote this book, in part, to explain to chief financial officers the financial (and non-financial) benefits of Lean management. In doing so, we hoped to remove chief financial officers as principal barriers to Learn transformation. We had a few successes, but not nearly as many as we had hoped for.

Throughout the history of progressive Lean management, its advocates have tried to do the same things over and over again to gain management's interest in leading broad, fundamental change in leadership routines and business processes. When we fail, we keep doing the same things, only harder. This has been a losing proposition and illustrates how guessing at the causes of problems does not lead to answers.

This outcome suggests that we should utilize structured problem-solving processes. Yet doing so will be difficult because the problem is comprised of dozens of variables that intersect each other in both predictable and unpredictable ways. We simply may lack a problem-solving process with enough capability to identify the "zero-day" flaw(s) in human information processing that would, if corrected, lead many more leaders to embrace Lean management.

Despite such limitations, we can still make meaningful progress. For example, when I meet with executives I often ask these two questions:

- What are your two or three biggest headaches?
- How long have they been headaches?

There is no hesitation in answering these questions. Invariably, their answers are related to information flow problems that have long been in existence, almost always internally, and often for decades – far more so than material flow or even sales or financial problems. Their answers obviously point to difficulty in both recognizing problems and lack of practice with structured problem-solving routines. But there is more to it than that.

Their answers reflect pain that they experience every day, like a splinter stuck in their finger that they cannot remove. While managers typically seek control, they have an abundance of information flow problems that they are unable to control. It is a source of constant irritation. This points to a different approach that might make Lean management more appealing to leaders: the human case for Lean management.

To my knowledge, the human case for Lean management has never been made. That is probably because people immediately judge it to be a feeble argument, without even considering what the human case might be. Herewith, I shall make the human case for Lean, and, further, show how the human case for Lean makes the business case.

We begin by totally forgetting the common conceptual foundation for Lean, which is to maximize customer value while minimizing waste. Free of this limitation, let's recognize the Lean management system as something different: a solution for information flow problems, and while we're at it let's turn all material into information. Now, instead of working mostly with money and discrete products or services, we work mostly with information and time. In this new framework, we would naturally become very concerned about the exchange of information in time. Let's explore this idea using a debtor, creditor, and asset analogy that uses information instead of money.

The obligations owed by debtors to creditors is an asset called information. The slow exchange of information (batch-and-queue) results in higher levels of debt compared to the rapid exchange of information (flow). The slow settlement of debt means that obligations between parties linger and are thus less satisfying. It disrupts and damages social relations as people are forced to behave in zero-sum ways to get what they want. The rapid settlement of debt is more satisfying because risk is reduced, as are the motivations for zero-sum behaviors.

Assume that the board of directors acts as the creditor who grants to the debtor, the president, an information processing asset to manage – the company. The president, in turn, becomes the creditor who grants to debtors, vice presidents, information processing assets to manage – the major parts of the company. The vice presidents, in turn, become creditors who grant to debtors, general managers, information processing assets to manage – smaller parts of the company. The general managers, in turn, become creditors who grant to debtors, middle managers, information processing assets to manage – even smaller parts of the company. The middle managers, in turn, become creditors who grant to debtors, supervisors, information processing assets to manage – the smallest parts of the company. The supervisors, in turn, become creditors who grant to debtors, employees, information processing assets to manage – a machine, part of a process, etc.

Employees who accumulate information debts (by withholding information, for example) are unable to settle with their creditor supervisors when they demand payment. Debtor supervisors, in turn, are unable to settle with their creditor middle managers when they demand payment. Debtor middle managers, in turn, are unable to settle with their creditor general managers when they demand payment. Debtor general managers, in turn, are unable to settle with their creditor vice presidents when they demand payment. Debtor vice presidents, in turn, are unable to settle with their creditor president when he or she demands payment.

The immediate outcome is that managers at all levels are annoyed much of the time, even if they don't realize it or act like it. The end results, predictably, are major problems in which capable managers are sacrificed for reasons unknown and likely unfair. Let's go back to the intermediate result, because that is something that we can impact. Will managers, being annoyed most the time, carefully evaluate information and make good decisions? Will they interact mostly in positive ways with people? Also, who wants to be annoyed every day at work for decades? Is that good for managers' health and the health those around them? What can be done about this?

Think about why employees withhold information, which exists as a structural problem in nearly every organization regardless of type or size. They do it for many different reasons, including:

- Fear of being blamed for problems.
- Unaware or unsure of what information to share and when.
- Fear of appearing to not be in control or lacking competence.
- A belief that information is not to be shared (knowledge is power).

Each of these can be corrected, but only if managers recognize them as problems and correct them by using structured problem-solving routines in non-blaming and non-judgmental ways. If they do that, they will recognize Lean management as an effective solution for information flow problems.

The business case for Lean, typically, focuses on increasing profits, etc., which can be achieved many different ways – all of which are far easier to do than to practice Lean management. So let's forget the business case for Lean; it is irrelevant to the primary interests of business leaders. The human case for Lean focuses on improving information flow, which can be achieved only one way. The human case for Lean, therefore, is more compelling than any business case for Lean.

Lean, done right, reduces and eliminates information flow problems and their myriad undesirable knock-on effects – which no leader can afford to endure. And, as I am sure you have surmised, information flow problems generate costs and consume profits. Who needs that in a period of low economic growth, or at any time?

Lesson 51

My Nikai Walks

The gemba walks I have taken over the years have always been interesting and educational. However, gemba walks are not the only type of walk I go on. For more than 15 years I have also taken nikai walks, which I find to be even more interesting and educational than gemba walks. Nikai (pronounced NEE-kai) is the Japanese word for "upstairs." Instead of going downstairs to the gemba, I go upstairs and take a walk through the brains of senior managers. I have gone on hundreds of nikai walks, and would like to share with you my observations as I wind my way through the different parts of the brain.

First, I get really small (my secret), then I begin my nikai walks at the brain stem. This part of the brain controls heart rate and breathing. Typically, there is nothing unusual going on there unless a stressor is encountered. I pass the cerebellum, which is responsible for motor control. This is an amazing ancient evolutionary chunk of tissue; one that looks a lot like a mini sfogliatelle. Its function is so basic and autonomous that there is nothing of significance to observe here.

Then I visit the temporal lobes, which are involved in emotion, memory, language comprehension, and hearing. This is where the fun begins. I find aged inventories of words and phrases that are inconsistent with Lean management. As might be expected, these result in poor word choices that make employees think that nothing at all has changed despite management's professed support for Lean. Abnormal sounds are heard regularly but they cause no reaction. Listening comprehension is often impaired as well.

Next, I go to the occipital lobe, which processes visual data. Here I find some problems. Visual data from the occipital lobe is comprehended by the temporal and frontal lobes in a way that makes everything that is happening look just fine. For example, people who are busy appear to be doing work, and people who work 10 hours a day appear to be working hard. Top managers cannot see what is actually going on because the visual data processing algorithm distorts the image. Their brain misleads them.

On to the parietal lobe, which integrates sensory information pertaining to body position, visual inputs, touch, etc. Overall, this area is usually in pretty good order, though a there are some important problems here too. One is lack of movement. Too much time is spent sitting in an office or conference room. Another is the lack of sensory touch, such as in getting one's hands dirty by actually doing the work. I also commonly find a deadening of the senses with respect to inputs coming from other people who experience pain or difficulties.

The frontal lobe is the most recent evolutionary feature of the brain, responsible for "executive function" such as planning, making comparisons, organizing responses to problems, speech, and decision-making. It is dense with dopamine receptors that signal pain or pleasure. The frontal lobe is constantly overloaded by never-ending streams of problems that arise from faulty business processes. As a result, the response to problems is mostly to blame people, which also happens to be the dominant relevant memory for both current and past experiences. The frontal lobe links to the orbitofrontal cortex and sometimes results in shouting or swearing when things go wrong – reduced forms of verbal and figural eloquence. I typically observe reduced empathy in this and other regions, sometimes to the point of being scary. I have also observed that logical and fact-based thinking is often overtaken by creative thinking. When this happens, politics trumps logic and facts, often to the detriment of one or more stakeholders.

Next, I do a quick walk through the olfactory bulb where odors are sensed. Periodically, abnormal smells are sensed but they cause little or no reaction. The smells are perceived as "just the way things are." So, in addition to abnormal sounds, abnormal smells exist in the workplace that go unrecognized and uncorrected. Nearby, but closer to the center of the brain, is the hypothalamus, which monitors blood pressure and controls appetite. It is common to find both blood pressure and body weight higher than they should be.

Further into the brain is the basal ganglia which is where deep memories and habits reside. Here I always find huge inventories of anti-Lean economic, social, and political ideas and practices that should be left for dead. It is where the senior managers' playbook resides, and includes such go-to habits as lay people off, close plants, and squeeze suppliers when problems arise. This is also the place where the habit of batch-and-queue information processing resides; a source of endless frustration for employees and other stakeholders.

Next comes the hippocampus which forms new memories and processes them for long-term storage. The hippocampus is also part of the limbic system, which regulates the human stress response (i.e. "fight-or-flight"). The hippocampus looks like a clam strip and kind-of smells like one fresh from the sea. Anyway, the hippocampus is a delicate feature that is easily damaged by long-term exposure to stress. Consequently, memory, as well as learning and creativity, diminish over time. It becomes much easier to tell people what to do, rather than think creatively, evaluate suggestions from others, or learn. I see this all the time.

The last stop on my nikai walk is always the ever-fascinating amygdala located deep within the brain. These little nuclei are quite unruly, constantly and selfishly focusing their host on basic survival. It is the seat of human emotional reaction and, as part of the limbic system, generates our millisecond response to threats. The amygdala is a troublesome part of the brain when it comes to business. It is a key player in the stress response, and initiates emotions and behaviors that are inappropriate for the situation.

For example, it drives senior managers to overreact and get upset over small problems, or it assures they are unreceptive, defensive, or even impervious to new ways of thinking and doing things. I always cut short my visit to the amygdala when this happens.

My nikai walks have taught me many interesting and useful things, and they explain why the gemba is usually in very bad shape. Another thing stands out: The human brain has not evolved much for business. It has great difficulty balancing the extant threats of business and personal survival (competition), the social obligations that help assure long-term success (helping, sharing), and the desire or requirement to achieve outcomes that must exceed actual needs. More often than not, the brain fails and then resorts to taking shortcuts in business that harm someone.

I have also gone on many nikai walks through the brains of talented Lean leaders; senior managers who do far more than passively support Lean management – they personally practice Lean every day. They managed to get out of the ancient amygdala information processing region and move to the new prefrontal cortex information processing region in the frontal lobe. Where nearly all other senior managers perceived uncertainties and threats, talented Lean leaders envisioned certainty and opportunity that was within their grasp.

The lesson learned from my nikai walks is that vastly different information processing routines appear to be what determines whether senior managers accept or reject Lean management. In short, the brain can easily mislead its host by misinterpreting information inputs, trusting previously established patterns, and favoring pleasure-seeking routines to defend against perceptions of pain.

Special thanks to Mark Jaben M.D. for reviewing and correcting this Lesson.

Lesson 52

Imitating Waste

Several years ago, I read an article about psychology researchers studying how young children, age three and four, learn compared to chimpanzees. The task for chimpanzees was to retrieve food from inside a container that was painted black so they could not see what was inside. The psychology researchers showed the chimps how to retrieve the food, but first they added unnecessary steps such as pulling a bolt back and forth and tapping the box several times with a stick. The most of the chimpanzees imitated the researcher's unnecessary steps. They did not understand the extra steps were unnecessary because they could not see inside the box.

Then, the researchers used a transparent box. The chimps could see the food inside and realized that pulling the bolt back and forth and tapping the box several times with a stick was not necessary. They went straight for the food.

Next, the transparent box was shown to children who were given the task of retrieving a toy from inside the box. First, the researchers did a demonstration: They put the toy in the box, did all the unnecessary steps such as pulling a bolt back and forth and tapping the box several times with a stick, and then removed the toy. They then put the toy back into the transparent box and told the children to retrieve the toy any way they wanted. Some 80 percent of the children imitated the researcher and pulled the bolt back and forth and tapped the box several times with a stick prior to retrieving the toy. They did not see these extra steps as unnecessary.

The results of this research indicate that humans learn by imitating other people, despite the fact that what they learn might be filled with unnecessary activities or steps – waste, unevenness, or unreasonableness. Importantly, if they do not understand the unnecessary activities or steps, few bother to ask a fundamental question: "Why must I do these steps?"

What I find particularly interesting about this work is the role of the researcher: They are an authority figure in the eyes of both the chimpanzees and the children, who may be weary of consequences if instructions are not followed.

In organizations, we also have authority figures: supervisors, managers, general managers, vice presidents, presidents, and CEOs. We know that most organizations process material and information via batch-and-queue, brimming with unnecessary activities and extra steps – waste, unevenness, or unreasonableness. Think of what happens in organizations when new employees are hired, particularly young people with little full-time work experience. Do you think most will do the work as they have been told to do it by their authority figure? You better believe it!

What happens if the young employee, or any employee, does not conform to the process or raises their hand and says to their authority figure that the process is bad? They are unlikely to get a prize. The more probable outcome is they get reprimanded.

Now, imagine people who have worked for an organization for decades and have seen the way other people do things. Their imitation of those routines are deeply embedded. As a consequence, they will usually resist efforts to do the work differently – that is, until authority figures start to do their work differently.

We know that the leaders of many organizations today advocate and support Lean, but they do not actually think differently or do their work differently. Few participate in kaizen, and therefore they cannot possibly understand Lean management. Their Lean tools training gives them just enough information to talk Lean, which seems more than good enough to them. However, the authority figures' failure to practice Lean means that employees have nothing to imitate. The result, always, is Fake Lean.

Recall the expression: "Imitation is the sincerest form of flattery." Authority figures are happy because they are in a no-lose situation. They are readily imitated by others seeking to imitate waste in both tasks and behaviors, just as they would be if authority figures were great models of Lean leadership.

The question becomes, do leaders want to create a workforce of skilled waste imitators, or do they want to create a workforce of skilled Lean practitioners? When the business is threatened, as it inevitably shall be, will a workforce of skilled waste imitators be able to save it?

Leaders often criticize academics as being "too theoretical." Yet, leaders who believe that their organization can "become Lean" without them having to understand and apply Lean principles and practices every day are operating under a theory that no academic would ever dream up.

Lesson 53

Lean Tinkers

Oh kaizen, dear kaizen, what has happened to you? This beautiful, human-centered process for learning, creativity, teamwork, and making improvements, both large and small, has been reduced to a yet another tool used incorrectly by managers. Lean thinkers? Hardly. Lean tinkers? More than you can imagine. How do I know this? Let me explain.

In the graduate-level Lean leadership course that I teach each semester, I ask my students, almost all of whom are full-time working professionals, the following question about kaizen: "How is kaizen understood and applied by senior managers in your organization?" Here are some of their responses (edited for clarity):

> "Senior management seems to allow kaizen rather than encourage it. As they see it, kaizen is an activity to be used by the operations team to fix problems. People use kaizen to fix specific problems, instead of for continuous improvement. Unfortunately, the director of finance has been able to squash ideas that have come from kaizen."

> "Senior management uses kaizen as a way of fixing the systems and processes that are not working, not to improve any and all processes. Kaizen is done in isolation. There will be a 'kaizen event,' then no review, or no time for continuous improvement. Senior management does not participate in kaizen or attend daily close-out meetings. Kaizen is reserved for operations and does not extend to finance or sales."

> "Kaizen is understood in my company as a fast, once-a-quarter approach to reducing cost. Kaizen is used

infrequently and never checked on to see if improvements actually stuck or could be improved even more."

"If kaizen occurs, most of the senior managers will ignore it or say it requires more money to make the changes. Middle managers have to fight with senior managers to do kaizen and implement the results."

"Their idea of a kaizen is to come to our shops and make changes they thought were necessary without any consultation from the people that work there. They don't believe in accessing the knowledge of the people who do the job every day."

"Improving processes is corrupted by the organization's goal save money. No attention is given to supervisor development or coaching, and it lacks top management support. Kaizen is job elimination under the guise of process improvement. They have failed to eliminate batch-and-queue processes."

"We are unable to do kaizen without the boss's approval. There is no reward for ideas. They blame people when processes don't work. Certain people are seen as problem-solvers, while the rest are seen as problem-causers. In this environment, few people make suggestions for fear of being blamed or losing their job."

"What we have are 'kaizen events,' which are just that; 'events' that have a start and end date with specific goals to achieve. Once the 'event' is over and the goals achieved, everyone involved gets a certificate and a round of applause, and that is the end of it. Our ops manager does mention that we all should continue and build on the improvements made, but

> expectations are not established and there are no follow-up discussions."
>
> "Managers don't support and attend the kaizen. They expect changes to be made by the group of people involved in the kaizen, which never happens, and management doesn't follow up. People think kaizen is a joke. There was a kaizen for changing around our whole area which was supposed to be attended by the president of the company, but was postponed twice due to conflicts which his schedule. When the kaizen finally happened, the president never attended or showed his face in any facet of the kaizen."
>
> "Senior managers don't understand kaizen correctly because they don't accept suggestion from others. They accept only their own suggestions."
>
> "In our monthly meetings, the workers get slammed publicly if they don't participate in kaizen."

This is wrong, all wrong. Who taught these managers kaizen? How did so many senior managers mangle kaizen? This seems more the result of management performed as a hobby rather than management practiced as a profession. This is not kaizen. It is something else and deserves its own name, one that reflects an activity that goes nowhere: "Möbius kaizen," after the Möbius strip, a one-sided surface with one edge.

Managers think they are doing something new and different with kaizen, but because they misunderstand and use it incorrectly the business ends up where it was before kaizen – lacking the ability to improve its processes. The general state of management and leadership remain unchanged as well. No learning has taken place, and kaizen has had no real impact in these organizations – other than to be seen as a joke or as a means to lay people off. Lean management requires curiosity and imagination. The few examples of REAL Lean that we have, and the many examples of Fake Lean, indicate there is very little curiosity or imagination among the leaders of organizations. As the above answers illustrate, kaizen is used by most senior managers to conform, not to transform people, processes, and the business.

If managers are not undergoing profound personal transformations in thinking and doing as a result of kaizen, like a caterpillar to a butterfly, then something is terribly wrong. As Art Byrne says, "Kaizen is good for you." I agree. However, that is true only if kaizen is understood and practiced correctly. Our collective, decades-long effort to create Lean thinkers – butterflies – among senior managers has fallen far short. Even the most optimistic among us must concede that. What we have done instead is create legions of Lean tinkers – we have been feeding hungry caterpillars that refuse to undergo metamorphosis.

We have a major failure to analyze, but A3 reports are inadequate because they do not examine managers' beliefs and untested assumptions, decision-making traps, and the different forms of illogical thinking that contribute to the observed effect. My A4 failure analysis method (see *Moving Forward Faster*, Appendix IV) is a much better choice for this type of problem.

I will ask my graduate students to analyze this failure and let you know the outcome. In the meantime, why don't you try to determine the root causes and identify practical countermeasures. Maybe together we can figure out how to transform legions of Lean tinkers into many more Lean thinkers.

Lesson 54

Imagination and Creativity

Like many others, I found my first experiences with Lean management to be personally liberating and the most fun I ever had at work. We were finally able to think "outside the box" as managers had for years requested, but never actually allowed us to do out of fear that we would cause trouble. Being allowed to think was a transformative experience. I could tap into my imagination about what was possible to achieve and generate creative ideas to get there. I made greater contributions to the company than ever before and I even felt better. I have not been the same since.

The lesson for me was clear: Lean requires imagination and creativity, which generates the bounty of ideas that are necessary to continuously improve processes, products, services, and people too. As a progressive system of management, it should not be surprising that Lean requires management capabilities that are absent in conventional management practice. And therein lies the challenge: People at all levels must think and do things differently from what they know or have been taught to do. The core vision behind Lean management is to get material and information flow. To make progress towards achieving that vision, the leaders of an organization must develop new beliefs, behaviors, and competencies, which, in turn, help everyone else learn and improve.

Senior managers must also be imaginative and creative in their leadership of the organization towards flow. They must be capable of imagining a target condition that represents, among other things, a much better place for employees to work. If not, then they will fail in the basic requirement to be a role model for others to follow. Lean without imagination and creativity results in bureaucratic Lean, as is often the case in large organizations, where people are required to apply Lean tools in order to qualify for some level of Lean accomplishment (e.g. certifications). Lean management has been reduced to a check-the-box program, though it does enable people to add many impressive-sounding things to their resume – but often without actually understanding the intent or meaning of the Lean method or tool.

The abundance of bureaucratic Lean, typically absent the "Respect for People" principle, indicates that imagination and creativity have been stripped from leaders. The lack of imagination and creativity implies conservatism and an unwillingness to try new things. That makes it difficult to re-conceptualize work and improvement processes, such as kaizen, as fun activities to engage in. The way Lean management exists in most organizations is to fit it onto leaders current capabilities (including hundreds of leadership process errors), rather than use Lean to develop new leadership capabilities. Lean should be used to create future state leaders who are more effective in their jobs and who make fewer errors.

Another thing to consider is the decades that most senior managers spend in chronically stressful batch-and-queue material and information processing environments as they rise through the hierarchy. The years of firefighting take their toll by changing the parts of the brain responsible for imagination and creativity, as does aging. It could be that some senior managers simply cannot summon the imagination and creativity needed to successfully lead a Lean transformation. This contributes to the prevalence of non-imaginative and non-creative bureaucratic Lean.

Imagination and creativity are fundamental to learning and problem-solving. It does not help when leaders characterize certain employees or departments as less important, unimaginative, or lacking creativity. This attitude leads to predictable outcomes: diminished learning and problems that linger unsolved for many years. The inability to engage the first step of the Scientific Method, to formulate a question (which lies on the premise that one can recognize that a problem exists), means the second step, to formulate a hypothesis or possible explanation for the phenomenon observed, will not occur. Problem-solving is cut-off at the start, and people are destined to deal with same problems over and over again. How unsatisfying.

Let's look at two examples where a lack of imagination and creativity assures the continued existence of terrible problems:

Example 1: A company constantly changes suppliers' schedules, sometimes several times a day. As a result, suppliers will not produce what their customers actually need, causing delays, shortages, and increasing costs. Does anyone recognize this as a problem? As a recurring problem? If not, cognitive capabilities (information processing) are obviously impaired. Therefore, people will not formulate a hypothesis to explain why suppliers' schedules constantly change. The inability to imagine costs and consequences and to creatively correct this problem means that employees will accept this abnormal situation – especially if senior management accepts it, which most managers do, typically for decades.

Example 2: Most senior leaders ignore the "Respect for People" principle because to them it does not seem to be where the money is. This is the result of being unable to imagine one's way out of the current state. It is also a failure to imagine how the "Respect for People" principle is fully responsive to the hard facts of business. Not just costs and profits, but also to enable continuous improvement (to achieve flow) and improve one's ability to compete on the basis of time. While senior managers want employees to be imaginative and creative, most do not set an example for others to follow.

The basis for any organization to adopt Lean management should be to transition from batch-and-queue material and information processing to flow through the imaginative and creative application of principles and problem-solving processes rooted in the Scientific Method. Leaders who understand this will experience far greater success than those who think of Lean management as nothing more than tools for cost-cutting.

In addition, senior management's relentless talk about cost-cutting – the persistent, negative, cut-cut-cut, never-good-enough perspective – demoralizes a workforce and inhibits employees' imagination and creativity. Instead, Lean management must be seen in its historical context as an uplifting way to improve the value proposition for customers and grow.

Lesson 55

The Amygdala Steals Our Lean Brain

This Lesson is an e-mail exchange with Mark Jaben M.D. (reprinted with permission of M. Jaben). In it, we discuss the neuroscience of Lean principles and practices.

By way of background, the overwhelming majority of our decision making occurs at the unconscious level, based on matching the various sensory inputs we experience with established patterns our brains have developed through evolution and experience. We are unaware of how fast these work and they are right most of the time, but may fail when there are new or novel circumstances for which there are no preexisting patterns. The conscious brain, the prefrontal cortex, fact checks the unconscious brain to be vigilant for these new or novel, outlier situations. However, the prefrontal cortex can only handle four to nine variables at a time, so it is easily overloaded. In addition, the prefrontal cortex constructs an explanation of the facts that seems plausible, but may not actually be true. Our conscious brain is not necessarily tuned into reality.

The amygdala, part of our unconscious brain, is our "flight or fight", stress response area, and when active, focuses us solely on the immediate threat in front of us. The amygdala is not about weighing options or discussing possibilities; it is about immediate action for survival. The prefrontal cortex is where we consider possible responses to threats.

• • • • •

Hi Bob – More neuroscience... The reason to move processing from the amygdala to the prefrontal cortex is the ability to engage in a dialogue, where various options and future circumstances can be judged, discussed and reconciled against the current circumstances, using the available patterns of recognition and then being vigilant for outlier conditions that don't exactly match the "rules." But to get creativity, there is literature to suggest the prefrontal cortex must be turned off. In essence, we must be able to move past the "rational" rules to get creative, out of the box thinking.

In one study, musicians were put in an fMRI and asked to read and play a piece of music. Then they were asked to improvise some music and a different area of the prefrontal cortex, the dorso-lateral gyrus, was now active, indicating that creativity occurs in a different part of the brain.

So how might we "control" this switch to a different brain area? In another study, researchers asked improvisational comedians what rituals they used to get ready before a performance. One person said they would strut around the dressing room making farting noises!

I have asked fellow musicians and performers and they each have a ritual before a show. So, what rituals might an individual employ in their working world to follow the rules when needed, but then move past them when creativity is needed. Importantly, what might I as a manager/leader put in place to foster and guide this ability?

In my own work in the emergency department, I continuously toggle between these two states- being creative when a patient's various complaints must somehow be amalgamated into their diagnosis, but following the rules once this is determined and treatment is begun – all while managing multiple patients in various stages of their individual process all at the same time.

I have noted that by recognizing the various value streams each patient enters, and then creating standard work that guides how I prioritize the work in process, I manage to reduce the overload on my prefrontal cortex and engage the creative part of my brain when needed. I don't yet fully understand my rituals though. (I

must admit I've not yet tried strutting around making noises representing bodily functions; there's enough of that already!)
I believe that kaizen is a ritual that does this. I also think standards are a ritual to help me recognize the outlier circumstances that then trigger the need to go to the creativity gyrus.

Hi Mark – You wrote: *But to get creativity, there is literature to suggest the prefrontal cortex must be turned off. In essence, we must be able to move past the 'rules' to get creative, out of the box thinking."*

People may be unable to get past the "rules" most of the time, which in this context means they can't turn off the prefrontal cortex because work is chaotic. The "rules" paradoxically generate lack of structure because they contradict one another, which consumes all of one's mental energy.

You wrote: "*I have noted that by recognizing the various value streams each patient enters, and then creating standard work that guides how I prioritize the work in process, I manage to reduce overloading my prefrontal cortex and engage the creative part of my brain when needed."*

It seems to me that the change from chaos to organization that you established via standard work allows you to be creative.
Kaizen allows people to organize their understanding of the process, rather than allow the process to exist in their mind as an amorphous or chaotic entity. I think we are saying the same thing.

My ritual prior to teaching or public speaking is to make sure I am organized; that I have everything I need and that I know what I am going to say. I work out the sequence, but not so much the timing.

Hi Bob – Yes, I think we are saying the same thing, namely, that the empiric experience that led to what we call "lean thinking" is, in fact, exactly what we are now understanding is the way our brains actually work.

By clarifying the chaos, we actually enable our brains to shut off the rules area when we identify an issue that goes beyond or is outside the bounds of the rules. Your pre-speech rituals, like those of the comedians and musicians, enable you to control where you are processing.

I find this helpful when I am dealing with staff, managers, senior leaders and other physicians in the hospital and patients. I try to figure out where they are processing during any given discussion and then try to move them to the brain area needed for what we are addressing. It is about understanding resistance (pushback), and working to overcome this in a kaizen spirit.

Hi Mark – Shit, we finally understand the way our brains actually work!

It is interesting how misaligned we are between how we normally think and conduct ourselves (e.g. chaotic batch-and-queue processing, contradictory rules, etc.) and how our brains actually work, which is better aligned with Lean principles and practices. The amygdala messes us up bad.

I've worked for nearly 15 years to align my teaching with Lean principles and practices, and find that students get a lot more out of the learning experience which they remember long-term and apply well into the future. So maybe the change from chaos to organization in a college course helps students learn better.
Perhaps this is an important way to move large number of people, over time, from batch-and-queue thinking to Lean thinking. Routinize Lean thinking in the structure and order created by Lean teaching.

Hi Bob – *"Shit, we finally understand the way our brains actually work!"* ----Well, maybe; I'm sure I'm oversimplifying it.

"Perhaps this is an important way to move a large number of people, over time, from batch-and-queue thinking to Lean thinking. Routinize Lean thinking in the structure and order created by Lean teaching." --yeah.

I think so; we are all so stuck in our amygdalas, which made sense thousands of years ago when we were being stalked by larger animals. But evolution is a slow process... for good reasons in many situations.

However, in these regards, too slow, but the saving grace is that as thinking individuals, we do have a prefrontal cortex, which we do use sometimes, and, when we do, we can learn and can adapt quickly.

On the other hand, maybe we are still being stalked by larger animals--ourselves.

What I continue to search for and understand is what exactly is/are the characteristics of a catalyst(s) that enable/allow a person to pause and consider an alternative world view - your classroom efforts are a good example.

Hi Mark – Perhaps oversimplifying, but close enough to have something one can work with, as you have shown. My classroom example suggests that one's attention needs to be captured for some time to generate an alternate worldview – particularly when it comes to comprehending Lean management vs. simply process improvement.

FYI, my amygdala is making me really mad!!! Despite a ton of effort, Lean progresses far too slowly.

Lesson 56

The Profits Generator

A while ago I had a spirited e-mail exchange with a well-known and highly accomplished Lean practitioner, someone I have been friends with for more than 15 years. The former executive, now a very successful Lean consultant, was responding to a Lean Leadership News article in which I criticized consultants for not making the "Respect for People" principle prominent in their work. They must teach "The Toyota Way," not "The Toyota Half-Way," I said. I would like to recount this exchange for you because there is much to learn from it.

My friend said to me that the C-level executives ignore the "Respect for People" principle because their overriding concern is profits, and so consultants have to focus on Lean tools and cost savings because otherwise they would not have a business. He said that consultants must deal with imperfect clients, and that they must understand the world from their customer's perspective. Also, he said that the "Respect for People" principle is typically addressed with the client after the contract is secured as they coach the client through their Lean transformation. He finished this portion of his feedback by saying that in the final analysis, the C-level's livelihood is based on profits, not on "Respect for People." That is their reality.

I do understand the C-level world-view and appreciate the demand the job places on them. I also understand there is an abundance of Fake Lean (incredible numbers of layoffs and other zero-sum outcomes), remarkably few examples of Real Lean, and that nobody is exempt from improvement no matter who they are or what their reality is. And, I understand it is the "Respect for People" principle that enables continuous improvement, not the other way around. Therefore, the "Respect for People" principle is the profits generator.

My friend, who has long misunderstood my work as being focused on "ideal Lean" or "pure Lean," suggested a better way for me to add value was by focusing on the transitional issues faced by these leaders. He thought my work would have greater impact if I addressed the issues that brownfield (existing) companies face, and I should understand the voice of the customer and stop demonizing C-level executives. If only I would put myself in into their shoes and understand their world.

My focus has been on "Real Lean" (applying both the "Continuous Improvement" and "Respect for People" principles), not "ideal Lean" or "pure Lean." Aspirational goals, if I have offered any, are practical devices to help people improve their performance; to guide them towards better outcomes. All 16 of my books speak to transitional issues in a brownfield environment, as do all the papers that I have written – all of which have appeared in practitioner-oriented journals. The brownfield is my background; it is the enduring frame of reference for everything I do. Other people write about greenfield Lean.

Rather than demonize C-level execs, I simply establish reasonable expectations of highly compensated people who choose to be in leadership positions, and who are responsible for the workplace and the livelihoods of other people. Holding a C-level position does not entitle one to deference or to stop learning how to be a better leader, just as being the best set-up man does not entitle one to continue doing 4-hour set-ups. Nobody is exempt from improvement.

Most people know that my writing is very direct. Some C-level executives may be offended by my writing, perhaps because I am close to the truth or because I challenge deeply held beliefs and assumptions. My friend appreciates that I have the fortitude to "say it as it is," because not too many people will do that. And, on second thought, he agrees that my writing offers practical transitional coaching to help C-level executives move from the current (brownfield) state to the future state.

I truly understand the importance of profits. So, I coach executives to learn, among other things, that the "Respect for People" principle is the profits generator and it must not be ignored. The "Respect for People" principle is what makes material and information flow, which, in turn, is where the money is. It is where the growth is. It is where the enterprise value is. And, it is where the C-level's livelihood is.

Finally, what about consultants? Historically, those who ignore the "Respect for People" principle have achieved far greater financial success than those consultants who have made it central to their work. That is because for a long time, customer demand for REAL Lean and incentives for changing how consultants go to market have been lacking, which, in turn, helps perpetuate Fake Lean (what I call "The Toyota Half-Way").

REAL Lean is, apparently, an ugly, unsellable product. Consultants, however, are great at finding ways to get customers to buy ugly products. So, go do your job. Sell REAL Lean. The future of Lean likely depends more on you than anyone else.

Lesson 57

Leadership Processes Reveal All

If you ask senior managers what they do on a daily basis, they typically cite a list of activities seemingly disconnected from one another. They view their workdays as highly variable in the type and number of activities they engage in. Most see their work as a collection of discrete activities distinct from larger processes. There may be exceptions, such as the budgeting process, in which leaders might view their role as part of the process rather than as a discrete activity.

I prefer to comprehend leadership as being made of many different processes, all of which must be operated under non-steady-state conditions (i.e. in dynamic, changing times). Understanding leadership from a process perspective is unusual and differs substantially from how leadership is normally studied and taught. Academic theories of leadership tend to focus on unique personal characteristics or the life stories of executives. This makes leadership subjective and more art than science. As a result, there are hundreds of definitions of leadership, most of which are leader-focused rather than follower-focused.

Employees also struggle to understand leadership from a process perspective. They perceive leadership as an ad hoc assortment of daily activities, even when the specific roles and responsibilities of leaders are fairly well defined. They generally accept this because they empathize with the time and job pressures that their managers face. While they certainly do not like poor leadership, they feel there is not much they can do to change it. The broader, chaotic business system drives their leaders to not lead or to take shortcuts that compromise effective leadership.

Because leadership is an observable phenomenon, it can be studied using the Scientific Method. Leadership is subject to cause-and-effect, which means that leadership problems can be understood and corrected using root cause analysis (5 Whys and fishbone diagram). Executives who are serious about improving their leadership skills and capabilities can practice leadership using a process such as the plan-do-check-act (PDCA) cycle. This makes leadership more objective and more science than art.

The process perspective of leadership is far more practical and fact-based. It has distinct advantages in that it does a much better job helping us comprehend leadership, and helps us realize that leadership is not the domain of the few people who possess unique personal characteristics such as charisma. Therefore, almost anyone can become an effective Lean leader.

The process perspective also helps us better evaluate leadership quality and effectiveness. It enables us to recognize the variation in how leaders operate processes that are common among them. Note that a leadership team would be intolerant of a work team where each individual operated the process differently. Yet in most organizations there is little or no actual requirement placed on a leadership team to operate their common processes with little variation.

The leadership variation that employees experience is often dramatic and contributes greatly to perceptions of poor leadership. This makes it difficult for employees to do their jobs and is a great source of daily frustration. In addition, if the quality of fundamental leadership processes is chronically low, then acute circumstances requiring intelligent, accurate, and strong leadership are likely to be absent.

What are the processes that leaders engage in? They include:

1. Leading and managing people
2. Planning and budgeting
3. Workload management
4. Decision-making
5. Problems recognition and response
6. Problem solving

7. Management reviews (finance, operations, HR, etc.)
8. Employee feedback and coaching
9. Team meetings
10. Asking questions, listening, and receiving feedback
11. Information sharing
12. Developing people
13. Performance appraisal
14. Walking around, "go see"
15. Stakeholder engagement (customer, supplier, investor, community)

Every large organization has informal or formal processes for each one of these activities. Despite this, the processes normally vary widely in quality and the time it takes to complete them. In most cases, each of these leadership processes are batch-and-queue.

As with any process, things can go well and things can go wrong. If many more things go right than wrong in each of these leadership processes, then we could characterize leadership as high quality and effective. Unfortunately, many things go wrong with each one of these leadership processes, in large part because they are batch-and-queue. Multiplied by the number of leaders in an organization, the number of errors can be enormous and its impact on employees widespread. It is unsurprising, therefore, that employees in most organizations are not satisfied with their leadership.

What are some practical examples of what can go wrong in these 15 leadership processes? What kinds of defects or quality problems can occur in these important and fundamental leadership processes? Let's look at them one-by-one and understand what can go wrong:

<u>1. Leading and Managing People</u>
Ignore employees, manage upwards, poor communication, confuse employees, unclear or unknown expectations, give orders, underutilize employees, demotivate employees, not

listening, micromanage, conflict, insult employees, disrespect employees, favoritism, not helping others, excessive ego or pride, assuming employees understand what you are saying.

2. Planning & Budgeting
Lengthy process, ignoring lower-level inputs, faulty estimates, misallocation of resources, non-allocation of resources, game-playing, given little attention, set people up to fail, lack of contingency planning, indiscriminate cuts, unrealistic schedule, ignoring problems, extensive re-work, across-the-board cuts, ignore marketplace information, keeping zombie projects alive.

3. Workload Management
None (pass-through), overload people, under-load people, frequent changes, everything is a priority, nothing is a priority, work misaligned with employee skills, lack of confidence in others, overwork high performers, under-work weak performers, assign too many projects, failing to provide assistance, poor estimates of time to complete, excessive pressure to meet milestones.

4. Decision-Making
Problem not understood, ignoring inputs, faulty assumptions, decision-making traps, illogical thinking, indecisive (delayed decisions, late decisions, no decision), political decisions, narrow-minded, flip-flop, hasty decisions, decisions based on flawed or incorrect information, other options not considered, results-focused, consequences not fully considered, address only symptoms of problems, unfair, unethical, immoral.

5. Problem Recognition and Response
Actual problem not recognized, ignore problems, procrastinate, incorrect response, blame employees (or suppliers) for problems, shoot the messenger, make excuses, fail to take responsibility, over-react, negative comments or body language, failure to "go see," firefighting.

6. Problem Solving

Ad hoc, sporadic, reactionary, inconsistent use of tools, ignore inputs, ignore alternate opinions, not asking for help, guess at causes, attribute problems to a single cause, fail to use scientific method, inaccurate or ineffective solutions, interfering, not being fact-based, politicizing problem solving, too busy to solve problems, resistance to change, not learning from others, not sharing with others.

7. Management Reviews

Perfunctory, unfocused, superficial, softball questions, blame or admonish for misses, praise for being lucky, focus on one negative event and ignore good work, hostile tone, require too many charts or slides, read e-mail during reviews, lengthy discussions on irrelevant items, favoritism, gamesmanship, politicking to look better than is actually the case, dishonest or inaccurate comments, frequently re-scheduled.

8. Employee Feedback and Coaching

None given, insufficient feedback, given infrequently, delayed, incomplete, inaccurate (no RCA), poorly prepared, biased, insincere, only criticism or only praise, lack of encouragement, lack of direction, feedback not specific, feedback not actionable, avoid or ignore difficult issues, bullying or abusive criticism, lack of respect, misjudge employee contributions, misjudge employee strengths and weaknesses.

9. Team Meetings

None or infrequent, re-scheduled often, start late, boss unprepared, disorganized, unfocused, no agenda, not following agenda, waste time discussing irrelevant matters, dominate the meeting, taking calls or e-mails during meeting, interruptions, one-way discussion, instill fear, employees afraid to speak up, always ask favorites to speak up, comments discounted or ridiculed, ignoring valid arguments, finger-pointing over problems, going off-topic, lack of ideas, not sharing problems and solutions, unproductive, re-scheduled often.

10. Asking Questions, Listening, Receiving Feedback
Not asking questions, confrontational or intimidating questions, fluff or irrelevant questions; trick questions, poor word choices, judging people, not listening, not taking any action items, misinterpreting, rush to reply, cut people off, blame people, distracted, de-valuing voice due to department or rank; insincere requests for feedback, ignoring feedback or suggestions, no follow-up.

11. Information Sharing
Perfunctory, late, batched and held in queue, inaccurate, incomplete, filtered, outdated, withheld, hoarded, secrets, unable to simplify to aid comprehension, sharing only good information, using information to harm others, withhold information to protect personal interests, bad information that leads to incorrect activities or actions, withhold information from those with a need to know.

12. Developing People
Not done, passive approach, general vs. specific development, incorrect development path, developing wrong people, training opportunities given to favorites, develop employees along narrow lines (to think or be one way), develop employees to "be like me" (vs. what the business needs), delegate responsibility to training department or to employees (self-development).

13. Performance Appraisal
Subjective, not fact-based, inconsistent application, variation in interpretation of appraisal criteria, unclear expectations, intimidating, biased (halo, leniency, similarity, central tendency, recency, favorites), re-scheduled often, political or ego-driven appraisals, non-constructive feedback, lack of fairness, inaccurate information to base appraisal, late, not completed, one bad incident anchors boss's entire view of performance, used to find flaws in people, used to degrade people, sustaining employees in pigeon-holes, poor understanding of actual performance (or boss's impact on performance), raise or bonus not connected to performance, lack of respect.

14. Walking Around, "Go See"

Never leave the office, make decisions based on reports, perfunctory visits to the workplace, no observation, no questions, does not understand the process, does not see problems, too little conversation, gets in the way, too much socializing, come out of office only when problems arise, micromanage.

15. Stakeholder Engagement

Ignore selected stakeholders, mislead stakeholders, not listening to stakeholders, insincere concern for customers, leave for others to do, unaware of or ignore critical feedback, lecture or criticize stakeholders, unethical treatment of stakeholders, blame stakeholders for problems, diminish stakeholder's interests, focus on only one stakeholder, lack of respect for stakeholders.

As you can see, a lot can go wrong. What are the effects of these leadership process errors on employees? Do these errors make them happy? Do employees ask for more errors, to make them even happier? Do these errors help focus employees' attention on their work and how to improve it? Do errors make them more creative and innovative? Do they put employees at ease? No, they do not. A hallmark of professionalism is a lack of errors, and that is not the case here. It is apparent that there are many opportunities for leaders to make errors, which generate many dissatisfactions among followers.

None of the errors listed are difficult or complicated for leaders to make. In most organizations, these are routine leadership process errors that occur day after day, month after month, and year after year. Executives would go crazy if workers made as many fundamental errors in the work that they do.

A key takeaway should be that leadership is an error-prone activity whose quality is normally very poor. This is at odds with our customary view of leadership as intelligent, thoughtful, and capable. As a result, leaders have much work to do to improve the quality of the processes that they engage in. Leaders who make few process errors will create more lively and engaged teams. Those who make many process errors will create a more dysfunctional social environment whose work product is poor.

The process perspective of leadership leads one to think about how to standardize leadership processes, much in the same way that value-creating work performed at lower levels is standardized (thus, establishing the basis for continuous improvement). The purpose for doing so, in both cases, is exactly the same: to improve quality, reliability, and effectiveness, and to reduce cycle times and costs.

There is one important difference between these leadership processes and the value-creating work processes that occur at lower levels in the organization: the presence of organizational politics. Imagine if organizational politics generated at lower levels heavily influenced value-creating work. It is certain that very little work would actually get done. Instead, people would fight with each other, focus their attention on the wrong things, and waste a lot of time. Left unchanged, the company would soon go out of business. Fortunately, leaders do not directly engage in value-creating work processes, so work does actually get done: goods and services are provided to customers on a timely basis and cash is received by the company.

Left out of value-creating activities, leaders do other things – often, busy-work such as meetings. Many will become deeply involved in organizational politics, which simply adds cost but creates no value. This will surely make life more difficult and slow down every person and every process. Why is this a problem?

It is a problem because organizational politics disrupts processes. To standardize the work that leaders do, and thus improve leadership processes, means that organizational politics must be greatly reduced if not substantially eliminated. This is not as difficult to do as one might think, once senior managers recognize that organizational politics generates mountains of waste, unevenness, and unreasonableness. Politics is a major distraction for managers that greatly impair an organization's ability to respond to customers and to changes in the marketplace.

The fact that there always seems to be so much opportunity for improvement reveals the existence of chronic abnormal conditions. The problems associated with batch-and-queue work processes divert management's attention from performing their leadership processes, and doing so with few or no errors.

Leadership process errors are not only bad for business, but they are also bad for the health and well-being of employees. The practical outcomes include:

- Confusion
- Distraction
- Time delays
- Inability to complete work
- Poor teamwork
- Reduced motivation
- Reduced loyalty
- Higher turnover
- Acute stress
- Chronic stress

Leaders make these errors, usually repeatedly, as if they have zero cost or consequences. To think that is true is to ignore reality. How can executives lead effectively if they ignore reality?

Understanding leadership as processes and understanding leadership process errors set the stage for huge advances in leadership capability and effectiveness.

To learn more about this, read the book *Speed Leadership: A Better Way To Lead In Rapidly Changing Times.*

Lesson 58

Professionalizing Management

People who are responsible for other people and processes are called "managers." Normally, people who hold such positions have deep knowledge of the subject matter. For example:

- Conductors know music
- Coaches know sport
- School teachers know subject
- Choreographers know dance

Oddly, most managers do not have deep knowledge of management. Specifically, they do not know about the management systems (and associated leadership routines), particularly flow in contrast to batch-and-queue processing. How can managers not know something as fundamental as that? It is the most basic aspect of daily life in organization, and which so profoundly affects the lives of employees, suppliers, customers, investors, and communities? It's not just their job, it's their profession. Or is it?

A profession is characterized by full-time employment in a discipline (knowledge area) and for which someone has received extended education and training. Management is indeed a unique knowledge area judging by the abundance of research and literature on the topic. And managers are usually employed full-time. However, they may not have received management education, such as an undergraduate or graduate degree in management, or employer-sponsored training. Yet, with few exceptions, formal educational processes do not inform managers about management systems – the ways in which material and information are processed, their strengths and weaknesses, and the specific ways people lead given the management system in use.

The absence of formal education and employer-sponsored training in management would qualify a manager as an amateur or hobbyist. For example, I was formally trained in materials engineering for 12 years and employed full-time in that profession for nine years. When I first joined management as supervisor, I soon realized there was an enormous amount that I did not know. I was a rank amateur when it came to management.

Recognizing this, I set out to simultaneously study and practice. I read hundreds of books and papers at nights and on weekends, volunteered for employer-sponsored management training and kaizens, and then applied what I learned in the workplace. The people that reported to me, then and in subsequent positions, knew I was doing this because I would often share what I learned with them. I provided evidence of my commitment to move beyond amateur status.

Many people have been or currently are in the same position I was. They left their profession as accountant, doctor, journalist, priest, engineer, or teacher and entered into a new profession: management. Some receive employer-sponsored management training, while others seek master's degrees in management or MBAs. While that is a good start, it seems that most managers who earn a degree stop there. The diploma, to them, means they have attained the requisite knowledge and are now done. That is incorrect. As a management professional and a role model, one must be committed to continuing education. Managers should be self-motivated to continue their study through ongoing research and daily practice (a professional PDCA cycle) because they are responsible for the workplace and for the livelihood of others.

It is because many managers do not educate themselves on a continuing basis that we find, even today, ignorance of Lean management, or, more fundamentally, a lack of understanding of the difference between flow and batch-and-queue processing. They also seem to lack awareness of how zero-sum behaviors (e.g. blame, politics) and zero-sum decision-making (e.g. squeezing suppliers, layoffs) undercut information sharing and teamwork that they so greatly desire. Can management, therefore, rightly be called a profession? If it is not that, what, then, is it?

Let's face it, most managers spend an extraordinary amount of time on the amateur aspects of the job – organizational politics, micromanaging people, blaming people for problems, ignoring suggestions, blocking ideas, protecting the status quo, etc., instead of the professional aspects of the job such as developing people, improving customer value, joint problem-solving with suppliers, eliminating waste, teaching, etc. They do this because they lack the education, training, or sensibility to realize how much damage the amateur aspects of the job cause over time to an organization, its employees, and other stakeholders. This suggests that a standard (i.e. target condition) is needed to help guide daily management practice. For that, we can use the Caux Round Table Principles for Responsible Business or copy Toyota's Corporate Social Responsibility policy.

In addition to this, there are many other practical things that can be done to improve this situation. Absent an A3 report, it is clear that some actions must be taken to professionalize management (and help improve capitalism, too). Four such actions include:

1) Managers must commit to educating themselves, in part because higher education often lags behind the needs of practitioners and academics typically do not have the work experience to teach the subject matter effectively. Managers should utilize the great information resources that exist to understand the differences between flow and batch-and-queue processing, including associated leadership routines.

2) Top leaders can establish a policy describing expectations for continuing education, self-

development, and daily practice for professional managers at all levels (including participation in kaizen).

3) Employer-sponsored management training should compare and contrast the differences between flow and batch-and-queue processing, and associated leadership routines.

4) Institutions of higher education should teach every undergraduate student the broad outlines of management systems and associated leadership routines, because nearly every graduate will work in organizations led by people who use a system of management to organize and execute value-creating activities. This could be a post-graduation element of continuing education, and summarized in as little as two pages front and back. It would make a nice visual control.

The word "professional" suggests someone who adapts and is progressive in their response to changing competitive conditions. Amateurs, however, are not likely to do that.

Lesson 59

Keeping Lean Management Alive

I think quite a bit about the long-term prospects of Lean management and ponder questions such as: Has interest in Lean peaked? How will Lean evolve in future workplaces less dependent on human labor? Will Lean die someday, or can prevent that from happening? I'd like to focus on the last question.

Progressive systems of management have fluctuated in prominence over time, increasing or decreasing in significance more-or-less in step with how people view progressivism in the larger social-political-economic context. A related question arises: How can interest in Lean management be increased in times where progressivism is seen less favorably? In my view, it is up to leaders of organizations to not "sit down;" they must ceaselessly move forward in order for Lean management to survive both locally, within an organization, as well as in the larger context.

"Continuous Improvement" is the phrase interpreted from the Japanese word "kaizen," which literally translated means "change for the better" (non-zero-sum, multilateral context). The changes made must result in improved outcomes, consistent with the "Respect for People" principle, which means, simply, to move forward. Continuous improvement means continuous forward improvement in response to changing circumstances. In addition, improvements must be made frequently so that the queue time between improvements is very small.

If continuous improvement begins to falter, then what emerges is discontinuous forward improvement because the queue time between improvements begins to increase. If discontinuous forward improvement stagnates, then fewer forward improvements are made and discontinuous backward improvement begins to appear – what we call "backslide." Discontinuous backward improvement accelerates, and, in a short time, years of forward continuous improvement are reversed. How did this happen? Leaders allowed continuous improvement to languish by lengthening the queue time between improvements; by people sitting down (both themselves and others). What happens next is remarkable to witness.

Good, effective improvements become aged over time and are no longer useful. They become the status quo. Soon, people begin to point to the aged improvements as evidence that continuous improvement does not work. People who were not part of the original improvement quickly agree and become vocal critics of the aged improvements, and, of course, see no connection to "Respect for People" that was once of central importance to the improvement made.

Yesterday's wonderful improvement becomes today's big problem. The empirical evidence cannot be refuted, their logic is iron-clad, and support builds for change – backward improvement. A return to the way it was, aided by a crisis if at all possible. Any crisis will do, even a small one, because leaders can easily inflate it. They will declare Lean management "obsolete." This call for change will be cited as evidence of good progressive thinking, but it is that only in name.

Everything learned and everything accomplished quietly recedes into the past.

I will never forget my many visits to The Wiremold Company when I was doing the research for the book *Better Thinking, Better Results* during the fall of 2001 through summer 2002. Every time I visited, often only a few days apart, things were physically or visually different. Kaizen, in its many forms, was taking place on a daily basis; continuous forward improvement. For most other organizations, however, making a few major improvements means that they are done. In reality, they are on their way to being un-done. They just don't know it yet.

Progressive Lean management will die by our own hand if it is understood as nothing more tools for manager's toolkit, and as cost-cutting, efficiency, or quality improvement. It will die by our own hand if we cling to the week-long kaizen "event" format and ignore the "Respect for People" principle or think it is automatically embedded in continuous improvement. It will die by our own hand when the queue time between improvements begins to increase – when we sit down. However, Lean will live long and prosper if we do not allow these things to happen.

Change for the better must keep pace with changes in the micro- and macro-environments, and it must be non-zero-sum (win-win). This is the way to reduce criticism that will inevitably come if improvements are allowed to become aged. It is our job, one-by-one, day-by-day, to keep REAL Lean alive.

Lesson 60

Surviving the 2-Sigma Economy

Graphs of economic performance in the United States over the last 150 years tell an interesting story of expansion and contraction. Since 1955, there have been nearly as many years of expansion as there have been of contraction. You can therefore say that the economy is broken approximately half of the time, yielding an economic system whose quality is about 300,000 ppm, or about 2-sigma. This is despite 500 years of economic study.

Imagine if a bridge that engineers designed and built a bridge failed, and then they rebuilt the bridge using the same faulty design only to see it fail again. Imagine if this process went on every five to seven years for 150 years. The engineers would be viewed as incompetent and unwilling or unable to learn from their failures. People would demand better engineering education and better engineering practice.

This does not happen when it comes to economics. You see, economics is a very big tent, and economists can survive and prosper whether they are right or wrong. Engineers, on the other hand, cannot survive and prosper when they are proven to be wrong. They must come around to correct ways of designing and building things or exit their field. What happens in engineering will probably never happen in economics because it is a social science, infused with politics and structural biases against seeing objective reality.

In addition, leaders' current knowledge of business and economics contributes to the 2-sigma economy and perpetuate is existence. This poses the question: How can organizations better survive, perhaps even thrive, in a 2-sigma economy? What can leaders do to better manage their business in such a macro-economic environment over which they have no control?

Leaders do, however, have control over their micro-economic environment – quite a bit, in fact. If the macro-economy is destined to go haywire every five to seven years (boom-bust cycles), the obvious solution is to become more flexible and greatly improve one's abilities to respond to changing circumstances. That means, they would transition away from supply-driven methods of producing goods and services, including the accounting and finance systems, metrics, policies, and procedures that support it. They would adopt a demand-driven method of producing goods and services, and the accounting system, metrics, policies, and procedures that support it. This would be a smart thing to do, if for no other reason that the organization's management system would be aligned with the competitive buyer's markets that they serve.

In order to actually become more flexible and greatly improve one's abilities to respond to changing circumstances, the leaders of an organization would have to commit to long-term capability building to become skilled at achieving flow (versus building inventories) and avoid the internal politics and reward systems that favor continued output even as demand wanes.

The only management system I know that can do this is Lean management. But the management system alone will not get the job done. Generations of managers will have to be trained in how to think and do things in ways that improve flexibility and the ability to respond to changing circumstances. Revolving-door leadership will have to slow, and management's focus must be on customer satisfaction as the means for creating shareholder value (vs. maximizing shareholder value) – and doing so in non-zero-sum (win-win) ways to avoid regression to supply-driven methods. It is a big job, but it is a fun job. Are you up for it?

Lesson 61

Beliefs Implicit in "The Toyota Way"

The Toyota Way 2001 is an internal document published in April 2001 by Toyota Motor Corporation to help covey to associates the elements of the company's culture that contributed to its success. The need to document Toyota's Way was due to Toyota's rapid growth and global presence, to help associates understand and advance it. Toyota senior management apparently deemed that there is much that others can learn from the 13-pages, and so it remains a tightly-controlled internal document. Generous as Toyota has long been, they do not feel the need to give to the world their source of competitive strength.

My view is that The Toyota Way 2001 document would likely have little or no meaning to most business leaders outside of Toyota. They will easily succumb to their biases or make excuses that the Toyota Way won't work for them because they are different. Apparently Toyota thinks *any* business can use it to develop their competitive strength and is unwilling to take the risk that others, however few, might benefit from it. While I agree that *any* business can use it to develop their competitive strength, but I think only a handful would actually do that.

I find that the explicit management beliefs and methods that the document refers to important and helpful for understanding, from my academic perspective, what made Toyota successful despite being a late entry into the automobile business. It also informs me of the fundamental mindset of that Toyota was able to transmit across generations of leaders – itself being a rare feat. Therefore, The Toyota Way 2001 document is significant with respect to the history and evolution of modern industrial management, a topic on which I have written extensively.

The Toyota Way (not to be confused with the Toyota Production System) is comprised of two pillars, which earlier pioneers of progressive management viewed to be core principles: "Continuous Improvement" and "Respect for People."

The elements that make up "Continuous Improvement" are "Challenge," "Kaizen," and "Genchi Genbutsu." The elements that make up "Respect for People" are "Respect," and "Teamwork." What follows below are my interpretations of the leadership beliefs that are implicit from my long study of the Toyota Way, and limited to the two principles and five associated elements that Toyota has made public.

CONTINUOUS IMPROVEMENT

Improvement is never-ending. Improvement is a daily activity. Continuous improvement is necessary to succeed in business.

Challenge

Long-term vision consistent with view that Toyota business is a long-term endeavor. It is people that meet the challenges through product/service and process creativity, not through money games (financial engineering or zero-sum actions).

Kaizen

Kaizen is a daily activity. Innovation yields competitive advantage. Success in business is mostly evolutionary, not revolutionary.

Genchi Genbutsu

Talking about problems is not good enough; you must get the facts. The most valuable information is obtained by going to the source - seeing, hearing, touching what is happening on the shop or office floor.

RESPECT FOR PEOPLE

People are valuable resources. Disrespect for people is creates waste, unevenness, and unreasonableness.

Respect

Respecting others establishes a foundation for successful interaction. Disrespecting others reduces mutual trust and creates resistance to new ideas and methods. Trust results in greater participation and satisfaction among Toyota people and other stakeholders. Trust is a mutual obligation. Building trust is everyone's responsibility.

Teamwork

People want to grow and improve. People want to work together and share. Both individual performance and team performance are important.

The Toyota Way 2001 expresses the explicit beliefs in how people best respond to challenges. The document is optimistic in its views and motivational, with a focus is on positive improvement (vs. negative cutting). It helps make people more accepting of change by removing fear, and motivates people to want to be part of something special. The "Continuous Improvement" and "Respect for People" principles are universal tenets responsive to the human condition. They apply to every culture, every stakeholder (both internal and external), every business, and every process. It reflects management's view that business must be a disciplined activity and rooted in the Scientific Method and common-sense beliefs and practices that support teamwork.

Contrast that with leaders who think the best way to respond to challenges is to lay people off, close sites, and squeeze suppliers; whose views are pessimistic and de-motivational (negative cutting, and more stick than carrot); instill fear, and de-motivate people, and make them part of something ordinary; use zero-sum principles that are non-responsive to the human condition; have a view of business rooted in the political method, weird theories, and zero-sum practices; and in a manner that diminishes teamwork.

Lesson 62

Gain Without the Pain

Lean management have always been more appealing to executives from a technical (financial and business metrics) point of view, than from a leadership perspective, principally because most executives do not think they need to do anything different. Their beliefs, behaviors, and competencies are seen as appropriate regardless of the management practice in use. They generally do not see Lean as requiring anything special of them, other than support and advocacy - neither of which place any actual demand on executives to think or behave differently.

It is difficult to tell executives that there are many, many new things for them to learn and do differently if they expect success with Lean management. Today, there are abundant resources (books, training courses, etc.) that executives can draw upon. Yet most executives are not book readers and most say they do not have time for training classes. If an executive does pick a book to read, the chances are great that he or she will pick one that reinforces their view that Lean is all about cost cutting and fixing processes, and that lower-level employees are the ones who must do that work. Lean training courses, in most cases, will carry the same or a similar message.

Some executives will see Lean as more than cost cutting and fixing processes, and are willing to become personally engaged. Soon they find out that Lean changes everything – including how they have long thought about economic, social, and political aspects of business – that is an instant deal-breaker for most leaders. It requires too much change in themselves.

I have found that most executives, much like anyone else, want all of the upside with little or none of the downside; the downside being their personal investment of time and energy into learning Lean management through the daily application of

Lean principles and practices – for years and years. They want improved business performance, credit for that outcome, and higher pay, but without having to sweat any more than they already do.

It is difficult to gain an audience for anything that is seen as causing too much personal pain (e.g. learning to behave differently) or as taking too long (e.g. learning to think and do things differently). However, even this reaction is useful because it informs us of who is not a good candidate to lead a Lean business. Unfortunately, the pool of executives not interested in Lean is much larger than the pool who are interested in Lean and willing take on big challenges, often late in their careers. Too bad the pool is so small, because the others don't know what great fun they are missing out on.

But more than that, leaders have a responsibility to lead, which means that they must do things they might not otherwise want to do or even hate to do. If a professional athlete were to have the same attitude and ignore improved ways of thinking and doing things (e.g. training), they would soon lose the ability to compete.

After many years of working on Lean leadership and reflecting on my work, that of others, and thinking about the many leaders I have interacted with, I find that the capable Lean leaders I have met possess the following characteristics:

- A musician's sense of time
- Curiosity of an explorer
- Humanity of a nurse
- Adaptability of a golfer
- Calmness of a teacher
- Skill of a martial artist
- Drive of an innovator
- Creativity of an artist
- Wisdom of a Zen adept

Maybe it is not so unusual that there are few capable Lean leaders. People do tend to be averse to pain. Those willing to put up with it deserve our admiration.

But, think about this: People in leadership positions are responsible for the lives and livelihoods of others. Therefore, they should be eager to endure the pain. If not, they are in the wrong job.

Lesson 63

Answers Hiding in Plain Sight?

My work has focused on Lean leadership since the mid-1990s. As a result, I have observed and thought much about what it takes to be an effective Lean leader. I have also given a lot of thought to why we have so few great examples of Lean management in organizations despite the effort of so many people over the last four decades. This brings me to three related questions, which you have probably asked as well:

- Why are so many organizations still ignorant about Lean management?
- Why do we have so much Fake Lean management?
- Why do we have so little REAL Lean management?

To refresh your memory, Fake Lean is the application of continuous improvement tools alone, and REAL Lean is the application of both "Continuous Improvement" and "Respect for People" principles and related practices.

I have searched hard for answers to these questions, chased dozens of leads, and uncovered hundreds of interesting and useful details. I learned a lot and share everything I know with others. Does my work provide specific and actionable direction that helps advance Lean among some top executives? Yes, it certainly does. But the three questions remain, and that bothers me. Once in a while the answer to vexing questions are simple and hiding in plain sight. Maybe this is the case for Lean management.

Below is a simplified characterization of executives that, based upon my experience, I believe to be broadly accurate. It places top executives into one of five categories, lists their percent in the population of executives (an educated guess), and includes a brief rationale.

Executive Diagnostic Characterization for Lean (EDCL)

Tired CEO / President	45%	Mentally or physically worn out by exposure to decades of batch-and-queue processing. Lean is OK for others to do. Abundance of Fake Lean and layoffs.
Don't Care CEO / President	40%	Talks about change, but actually prefers status quo and stability for self and others. No REAL Lean; little or no Fake Lean.
Psychopath CEO / President (sub-criminal)	5%	REAL Lean does not satisfy them in any way (loss of control, fear of failure due to insecurities). Accepts Fake Lean to gain power and conrol over others. Forces Lean tools onto people and lays many people off.
Don't Know CEO / President	9%	Enthusiastic about change and Lean, but does not know how and can't find the time to to learn or find people who know how.
Enthusiastic CEO / President	1%	Likes to learn and try new things. OK to be and think different. Personally engaged. Strong evidence of REAL Lean.

It is not intended to blame or praise anyone, but only to describe a phenomenon. While no executive would openly admit to being in either of the first two categories, I think they capture the actual situation deep beneath the surface. Finally, the key assumption for the EDCL is that Lean management has to be led top down, and there is ample empirical evidence to support that.

Assuming the EDCL is approximately correct, what does it tell us? More specifically, what does it say about where we should focus our efforts to advance REAL Lean management?

You can image that after 30 or more years of dealing with the problems generated by batch-and-queue material and information processing, many executives would, deep down, be physically or mentally exhausted. Who can blame them? While Boards of Directors should always find leaders who have great energy, no matter what their age, it's probably easy for candidates to fool the Board into thinking that they have lots of mental and physical energy. It seems reasonable that they would readily adopt Fake Lean as something for other people to do; those who have much greater mental and physical energy to improve core business processes. The "Tired" executives simply replace their weakness with someone else's strength, and let them do the hard work of Lean thinking and Lean doing.

What about the "Don't Care" CEOs and presidents who are more interested in status-quo and stability, and making sure things do not fall apart during their tenure? Maybe we should focus our attention here and convince some of them that they should care, and that Lean will not make things fall apart. However, we have to realize they are the ones in standing in harm's way (rivals, Board of Directors, shareholders, media, etc.), not us. They likely would not be receptive to taking what they will perceive to be big risks at the pinnacle of their career. For most CEOs and presidents, that's not in their plan and will never be.

The psychopath CEO or president is a big problem for us and for everyone else. While perhaps not great in numbers, they do an incredible amount of damage to people and to Lean management itself. Hopefully Board of Directors conduct good background checks to weed out psychopath CEOs and presidents. But we know empirically that this too is wishful thinking (most of the time). Psychopath CEOs and presidents will never be interested in REAL Lean, though most will use Fake Lean to satisfy their own needs to control people. We surely have no audience here.

Then comes the "Don't Know" CEOs (category and description by Kevin Meyer). They care a lot about their people, their customers, and the company, and know that there are better ways to do things. They also know there are people out there who are smarter than him. They have likely read about and comprehend the power of Lean. They want to be REAL Lean leaders but do not know where to begin.

What about the 1 percent category? It means that Lean management, REAL Lean, appeals to very few people. While that may not be what we want to hear, perhaps the market we have for Lean management is exactly what it should be: about 1 percent. If that is indeed true, then we should focus our more of efforts on the 1 percent of current and future top executives who are enthusiastic about Lean and help them.

In summary, it seems that we should be able to find an audience among a small percentage of the "Tired" executives, a larger percentage among the "Don't Care" executives, and an even larger percentage among the "Don't Know" executives. We know from experience that "Enthusiastic" executives are largely unsuccessful at convincing the "Tired" and "Don't Care" executives of the merits of REAL Lean management. So we should not waste their time asking them to convince others of the merits of Lean. Their time is better spent at work. But we also know that the "Tired" and "Psychopath" executives are very influential at convincing others to adopt Fake Lean. How can we modify or stop that?

This raises some important questions: What strategy can be used to develop interest in REAL Lean among some of the "Tired" executives? Would the strategy be different for the "Don't Care" executives? What can we do to better support the "Don't Know" and the "Enthusiastic" 1 percent? What about consultants? Who do you think they like to target for Fake Lean – "Tired," "Psychopath," and "Don't Know" executives? Can we do anything about that? Should we even try?

Lesson 64

Lean Tools: Blessing and Curse

"Lean is one amongst many tools available to any organization to remain competitive."

This quote illustrates a fundamental problem: People look for something that can help them with their immediate problem while completely missing the bigger picture – often for decades. People see Lean as tools, roughly equal to any other tool that helps solve a problem and improve competitiveness, rather than a comprehensive system of management. This narrow perspective mischaracterizes Lean and misinforms people.

Lean tools are relatively easy to understand. Most have been around since the early days of industrial engineering (though Lean tools can also be easily misunderstood and incorrectly applied). Lean management, on the other hand, is difficult to understand. It is a challenge to recognize and understand the interconnections between the two Lean principles and each of the Lean tools. Most people do not think about this, and so they end up cherry-picking the tools to suit their needs. While their heart might be in the right place, the results are far removed from Lean management.

Cherry-picking has been a problem for more than 100 years. In recent times, there are legendary examples of Fortune 500 corporations cherry-picking Lean to create their own custom operating system. What they invariably end up with is Lean-lite, or no Lean at all, and call it the "(insert company name here) Operating System." It is good that they name it something different because it no longer bears much resemblance to Lean management.

Lean management is difficult to understand because it is a non-zero-sum (win-win) management system. Contrast that to conventional management, which is zero-sum (win-lose) and is extraordinarily easy for people to understand and do. I win, you lose; it's simple, just as it is in sports or in war. However, business is not a game or a war. Creating losers invariably means that stakeholders will, sooner or later, start to work against the organization's interests. The result, for certain, will be increased costs and delays when action is needed.

There are many examples of human endeavor that are zero-sum, so it is not hard to see why most executives would see business that way. Plus, after 20 or 30 years of practicing business in a zero-sum manner, most executives find non-zero-sum business almost impossible to comprehend let alone put into practice. What does make perfect sense to them, however, is the application of Lean tools in a zero-sum manner. Lean tools are used as a stick, not as a carrot. Lean exposes the weakness of conventional management, which few leaders willingly wish to confront. Hence, the popularity of Fake Lean.

Think how much better business could do for itself and its stakeholders if senior managers were non-zero-sum. For Lean management to spread and prosper, it must gain populist support. Meaning, workers must understand Lean management as non-zero-sum and something that helps improve their workplace. They must embrace it and advocate for it, which in turn will push senior management towards Lean. However, Lean will never gain populist support if management always uses Lean in zero-sum ways, principally to make the numbers short-term.

This highlights the importance of Lean training, both classroom and on-the-job. However, most so-called "Lean Leadership" training for senior managers is classroom-based and focused mainly on Lean tools, and therefore does not result in the creation of Lean leaders. It is necessary for leaders to know Lean tools, through training and practice, but it is not sufficient. For leaders, it is far more important that they first understand the economic, social, and political aspects of Lean management, and also learn history's lessons.

Lesson 65

Kata Vision

Mike Rother has done us all a great service by informing us of the 4-part improvement kata and the 5-question coaching kata models in his book, *Toyota Kata.* Disciplined use of these katas can only help people move towards their future state. I really like the coaching kata. However, there is one aspect of the improvement kata that concerns me: the vision.

The improvement that people work on depends upon the vision. If the vision is flawed, then the resulting improvement kata becomes a counterfeit or fake improvement kata. Practicing the improvement kata gives the appearance of improvement, but improvement is being made towards a flawed challenge. This will surely cause problems.

I often find that executives who have embarked on a Lean transformation, but who remain steeped in conventional management, select company-level visions that reflect conventional management aspirations such as: to be number one in sales; meet certain financial targets regardless of economic environment; operational excellence; grow 20 percent per year, etc. The improvement katas that emerge from these visions often lead to the dysfunctional pursuit of certain business metrics to please only one stakeholder: shareholders.

In most cases, we can expect senior managers, even those who know Lean management fairly well, to do a poor job with regard to establishing the improvement kata vision(s) for the company because they will often revert to the zero-sum (win-lose) mindset of conventional management. It is what they know best, and this usually means poor outcomes for employees, suppliers, customers, and communities.

So a word of caution: A lot of thought must go into the vision for the improvement kata to actually result in improvement that benefits all key stakeholders in non-zero-sum ways. While this is particularly true for company-level challenges, department- and division-level visions must also be carefully thought through by management. My book, *Moving Forward Faster*, will serve as an excellent guide for you to avoid fake improvement katas.

If future economic success depends upon the workers' minds more than their muscle, then leaders have to commit to the long-term development of human intellectual capital. They must not mess with workers minds, causing annoyances and distractions that reduce creativity and innovation. Give the people what they want: employment, development, advancement, wage increases, benefits, and peace of mind. Management's kata visions must reflect this. Leaders should not need unions to force them do these things.

Lesson 66

People and Processes

When people get together to do work, they almost always do two things. One is technical, the other is behavioral:

- Technical: Process material and information using the batch-and-queue method.
- Behavioral: Create hierarchies and organizational politics.

As a result of batch-and-queue processing, processing times are short while queue times are long in duration. Thus, it takes a long time to complete a process or activity. Because batch-and-queue processing works, few people see the need for flow. Yet, everyone must live with the technical consequences:

- Slow response
- Many processing steps
- Many errors
- React to problems
- Delays
- Re-work
- Long hours
- Rigidity
- Results-focused

They must also live with the behavioral consequences:

- Complex
- Chaotic
- Confusing
- Unpredictable
- Illogical
- Politics

- Lack of control
- Blame people for problems
- Zero-sum thinking and decisions

Importantly, these behavioral consequences result in blocked information flow and stifle creativity and innovation among employees. Not only does the company and employees have to live with these unfavorable behavioral consequences, but so do other key stakeholders: suppliers, customers, investors, and communities. Batch-and-queue processing generates problems that are shared among the stakeholders. In addition, both the technical and behavioral consequences of batch-and-queue processes are entwined with the numerous leadership process errors described in Lesson 57.

In Lean management, we apply kaizen repeatedly to convert from batch-and-queue processing to flow. Recall the three principles of kaizen:

- Process and results
- System focus
- Non-blaming, non-judgmental

As a result of kaizen (done right), batch sizes are reduced, queue times are shortened and eliminated, and processing steps are combined and eliminated. Thus, the process has been improved – without speeding people up – while at the same time improving quality, reducing lead-times, and lowering costs.

The technical consequences of Lean management include:

- Rapid response
- Fewer processing steps
- Fewer errors
- Avoid problems
- Fewer delays
- Less re-work

- Normal hours
- Adaptability
- Process and results focused

The behavioral consequences of Lean management include:

- Simpler
- Orderly
- Clear
- Predictable
- Logical
- Reality
- Control
- Praise people for problems
- Non-zero-sum thinking and decisions

These behavioral consequences enable information flow and promote creativity and innovation among employees. These behavioral consequences are far more favorable to suppliers, customers, investors, and communities.

The difference between batch-and-queue processing and flow is remarkable, even if only from these perspectives. It is important to recognize that batch-and-queue processing and flow are completely separate knowledge areas, much like neurology and orthopedics. So much more can be said about the benefits of Lean (done right) and the competitive advantages that it can deliver. However, we must return to batch-and-queue processing to examine it more deeply and better understand its impact on the health of employees.

Given the technical and behavioral nature of batch-and-queue processing, what type of manager is likely to be attracted to it, and who might be repelled by it? We know that the problem-rich, error-prone batch-and-queue environment necessitates micro-management and constant interactions with people. Who would like to do that?

Introverts, especially strong introverts, generally have little interest in dealing with people. They typically avoid management positions and prefer to be individual contributors. If they do become managers, they are often bad managers due to their inattentiveness to people issues. Doing that type of work does not excite them.

Extroverts, on the other hand, are stimulated by dealing with people. They would be attracted to batch-and-queue environments, and may be either good or bad managers in such environments. It depends upon how they react to the technical and behavioral consequences of batch-and-queue processing.

Psychopaths, however, enjoy making people miserable. It is their primary source of stimulation. Psychopathic behaviors include degrading comments and insults, intimidation, bullying, anger, condescension, biases and stereotypes, manipulating people, public humiliation, aggression, fist-banging, yelling, cursing, throwing objects, revenge, lying, ostracizing people, setting people up to fail, backstabbing, etc. These are examples of behaviors that add cost but do not add value.

The batch-and-queue environment is a wonderful place for them because it offers so much opportunity to make people miserable. If a crying baby can induce an acute stress response in a loving parent, what do you think a yelling supervisor does to employees? What if the supervisor yells at employees all the time? What greenhouses are to plants, batch-and-queue businesses are to psychopaths: a warm and comfortable environment to thrive in.

Let's not forget that managers do not add value to the products and services that a company supplies. Thus, they have abundant time every day to make subordinates miserable, especially those leaders whose focus is almost singularly devoted to achieving results – mainly, financial (or numerical) results. This, too, favors the interests of psychopaths.

Of course, not every senior manager is a psychopath, but they may be driven towards psychopathic-like behaviors in the pursuit of business goals in batch-and-queue environments. Psychopathic bosses generate enormous amounts of technical and behavioral waste, unevenness, and unreasonableness. Recognize also that I do not mean to imply that flow environments will be completely free of psychopathic managers. However, the flow environment is far less accommodating of their interests. The "Respect for People" principle is a repellent to psychopaths.

The problems associated with psychopathic senior managers are innumerable, but I'd like to focus on just two: time and stress. The effect of bad leadership behaviors on organizations is to change the nature of time. The clock normally reads in hours or seconds. But complexity, chaos, confusion, politics, blame, etc., slows down the clock so that it reads in hours and days. In highly political, blame-oriented batch-and-queue environments, the clock further slows to weeks and months.

Executives have force-fed politics to everyone in the company – a giant Quaalude (methaqualone, a sedative-hypnotic drug) that has sedated the company and greatly slowed down both people and work (even though people seem to be very busy). The outcome is an inability to see reality, reduced responsiveness, delays in decision-making, poor adaptability to changing circumstances, and difficulty competing. These are common characteristics of batch-and-queue environments. Another outcome is the creation of an environment of chronic stress for employees at all levels. Batch-and-queue processing lead to environments with these well-known characteristics:

- Unknown expectations
- Non-specific criticism
- Micromanaging
- Dysfunctional teams
- Endless meetings
- Presentation after presentation

- Authoritarian bosses
- Hierarchy (status differences)
- Formal protocols
- Resource starvation
- Do-as-you-are-told (don't think)
- Unreasonable deadlines
- Illogical decisions
- Dysfunctional performance reviews
- Results focus
- Blame people for problems
- Constant threat of unemployment, etc.

These too are entwined with the numerous leadership process errors described in Lesson 57. Simply put, it is a stressful and frustrating work environment. Yet, these are not the only stressors that employees are subjected to. They also have many stressors in their personal lives such as:

- Spouse
- Being a single parent
- Children with problems
- Special needs children
- Childcare or eldercare
- Illness
- Financial issues
- Time constraints
- Mortality, etc.

These stressors give employees the constant feeling that they are threatened, and, in response, they mentally "run for their lives." The lack of control and predictability in their work and personal lives generates stress over the long-term. The lower the social standing of the employee in the company, the less control they feel they have. This is not the result of overactive imaginations. Most leaders of large companies perpetually subject wage earners and salaried workers to the threat of layoffs and outsourcing, even when the business is profitable and economic times are good. As a result, workers do not trust their leaders.

The stress response is how animals physiologically react when their lives are threatened. It is the automatic fight-or-flight response activated under conditions of acute stress. A zebra will generate a stress response to marshal all of its biological resources to avoid being eaten by a tiger. If the zebra avoids capture, the stress response fades and it returns to its normal rest condition state.

Like zebras, humans will generate an automatic fight-or-flight response under conditions of acute stress. However, humans are different from other animals in that we can feel that our lives are threatened by things that will not actually cost us our lives. For example, getting yelled at by the boss does not kill us, but we respond to it as if does. Likewise, an argument with our spouse does not kill us, but we respond to in it as if does. We can also activate the stress response just by thinking of financial problems, being late for an appointment, rushing to catch an airplane, presidential elections, the price of gasoline, or our child's future.

The stress response is a millisecond response generated by some event that is perceived as a threat. We react before we realize what is going on. Have you ever been in a meeting and felt threated by what someone said, only to realize a moment later that the person was not actually picking on you? The stress response kicked-in before you fully understood the context of the conversation. That is an example of an acute stress response. The physiological effect of the stress response is to immediately put the body into survival mode:

- Pupils dilate
- Dry mouth
- Perspiration increases
- Breathing increases
- Heart rate increases

- Increased blood flow to muscles and brain
- Digestive activity is inhibited
- Liver releases glucose (for energy)
- Kidneys release stress hormones, epinephrine and norepinephrine (i.e. adrenaline and noradrenaline)
- Bladder relaxes
- Rectum contracts
- Immune system suppressed

There are many situations where acute stress may occur in the workplace and thus trigger the stress response. While we may not like the feeling of the stress response, no lasting harm is done. The big problem comes when threats in the workplace result in chronic stress, where the stress response is always "on." The batch-and-queue environment is a perpetually threatening environment for workers: unstable processes, volatile managers, and layoffs, to name a few. People low in the hierarchy will feel less in control and be more affected.

Chronic stress results in the continuous release of stress hormones. This accelerates the aging process and slowly kills people. High levels of glucocorticoid (a steroid hormone) and epinephrine (adrenaline) in the blood stream for prolonged periods of time are bad for one's health. Workers marinating in high levels of stress response chemicals develop serious medical problems such as:

- Atherosclerosis
- Hypertension
- Abdominal (visceral) fat
- Chromosome damage (telomeres unravel)
- Weakened immune system
- Hippocampal atrophy (learning and memory center in the brain)
- Neuron (nerve cell) damage
- Fear

- Anxiety
- Depression

We must also remember that chronic stress often leads to poor nutrition. People will consume unhealthy foods and drinks to deliver comfort and provide temporary relief. Poor nutrition, as well as a lack of physical activity, will contribute to these medical problems.

What is the effect of these medical problems on employees in the workplace? Over time, they will have greater difficulty performing their work due to physical and cognitive limitations. The will be sick and out of work more often. They will seek simpler tasks, and their contributions will diminish. These are, of course, avoidable outcomes, but not if executives continue to possess an incorrect view of Lean management.

Unfortunately, most executives think Lean is nothing more than the addition of some proven productivity improvement tools to their management toolbox. They like the "Continuous Improvement" principle but ignore the "Respect for People" principle – the enabler of flow. Therefore, batch-and-queue processing still exists, with all its problems cited at the beginning of the Lesson.

Not only that, leaders who subject workers to chronic stress in the workplace exhibit the ultimate disrespect for people: wasting their lives. They do this not only from a health perspective, but batch-and-queue processing has people do many things that are not necessary to do. One way or another, workers lives are wasted. Is that the role of management?

This begs an important question: What is management's responsibility to ensure a workplace that is safe from chronic stress due to its severe effects on human health? We know senior managers are responsible for physical health and safety of workers. If chronic stress results in physical health problems, then are executives also responsible for workers' mental health as well?

What about workers? What are they responsible for? Is it up to them to manage their stress response? Should they simply take deep breaths when a supervisor or executive triggers a stress response? Should the company offer stress management training, thereby addressing symptoms rather than root causes? Should workers who don't like the environment simply leave the company and find jobs elsewhere? Is this a good way to develop and retain an organization's best people?

Obviously, the employer has the brunt of responsibility because they have the power. Management is in charge and has a choice as to whether or not it operates an unhealthy, dysfunctional batch-and-queue system for material and information processing.

Executives complain a lot about the high costs of healthcare, which feeds the perception that people are always the problem and leads to expensive strategies to replace or eliminate employees (e.g. outsourcing, offshoring, computers and software, robots and automation, etc.). For all their grumbling about the high cost of healthcare, most executives take no personal responsibility. They see no connection between how they lead and its effect on the mental and physical health of workers.

Executives should compare the list of medications used by employees to those medications used in the general population. Are medications for illnesses related to chronic stress and stress-related illnesses are greater in the company than in the general population? If so, then that should inform them that something is seriously wrong with how they are leading. It might also suggest a high tolerance for the existence of psychopathic managers.

Let's assume there is no correlation between medications used by employees and the medications used in the general population. Does that mean everything is OK? No, it does not. Fundamentally, batch-and-queue material and information processing is more resource intensive than flow, and technical and behavioral waste, unevenness, and unreasonableness abound. Organizational politics, the big Quaalude (the central nervous system depressant), slows down decision-making and responsiveness to changing circumstances. And there remains significant individual and organization weaknesses when it comes to creativity, innovation, and competitiveness.

Because of organizational politics, batch-and-queue environments also readily create in-groups and out-groups – meaning, social inclusion and social rejection. This affects the ability of employees to socialize across boundaries and develop supportive relationships. Social rejection, of course, is a source of mental and physical pain. Supportive social relationships (e.g. real teamwork versus fake teamwork) in organizations have a positive health benefit. Executives need to make their employees feel wanted and appreciated (vs. disposable).

Knowing that co-workers and managers are trustworthy helps people avoid wasting physical and mental resources on stress responses. The challenge for executives, which most ignore, preferring to focus on the numbers, is to improve the social condition within the workplace. Think of it this way: As a golfer, you can drive the ball really well, but your short game is very poor. What should you work on if you want to improve your golf game – driving, or chipping and putting? Business is not a game, but this example illustrates that executive capabilities, in most cases, are gravely incomplete.

Psychopathic managers – CEO on down – should be identified and given training and support to improve, moved to independent contributor positions, or discharged from the company as appropriate. These actions must be taken even for those managers who are judged as the most effective. Managers at all levels must learn a new path for success, one in which they will surely feel better about themselves and their accomplishments. They must learn how to eliminate technical and behavioral waste, unevenness, and unreasonableness. Playing trumpet was good while it lasted. It is now time to learn how to play drums.

Lesson 67

Healthcare In Lean

Today it is increasing common to find Lean management in healthcare organizations. This is a noble cause, and one we will all surely benefit from if Lean is practiced correctly. In this Lesson, we will examine the opposite of Lean in healthcare: healthcare in Lean. By that, I mean how Lean principles and practices (methods, processes, and tools) deliver positive health benefits to people in organizations that practice Lean correctly.

Executives have many responsibilities. One prominent responsibility that is usually not recognized is to set employees up to succeed. It is more likely that managers set employees up to fail (see Lesson 57) – not all employees, and not all at once, but certainly many employees and at numerous points in their careers. Ill intentions may not be present, yet the outcomes are still bad for employees.

Leaders who want to be served by employees ask different questions than leaders who serve employees. For example, servant leaders will ask themselves what they can do to set employees up to succeed. They ask: "How can I help you?"

Think of it as the challenge faced by field-goal kickers in football. A coach who asks the kicker to attempt an 80-yard field-goal has set his kicker up to fail. The range of the kicker is 50 yards or less, depending upon field and weather conditions. The closer the kicker is to the goalposts, the greater the probability of scoring three points. So, the coach calls plays on offense to get the kicker closer to the goal posts. Despite best efforts there will be misses, from which important lessons are learned and applied to future offensive plays and field-goal attempts.

The correct use of Lean principles and practices are like well-executed offensive plays that move the kicker (employees) closer to the goalposts. They improve the kicker's probability of success. Or, you can think of Lean principles and practices this way. They make the goalposts look larger to the kicker, even if he is far away. Either way, the probability of success is improved.

Executives should be working hard to set employees up to succeed by eliminating technical and behavioral waste, unevenness, and unreasonableness. To do this they have to learn the new language of flow, which will make them smarter and also help them to become complete executives. They must do this in ways that improve employee's physical and mental health. It is notable that environmental health and safety departments in most corporations focus only on the physical health and safety of employees and have yet to incorporate mental health and safety into their responsibilities. They should do this immediately.

Management's goal should be for employees to leave work each day healthier than when they arrived.

How do Lean principles, methods (processes) and tools deliver positive health benefits to people in a company? Generally, their effect is to help employees see reality and give them measures of control and predictability that they cannot get by any other means – even for people low in the hierarchy. Work is more focused, with less need for multi-tasking, and creates conditions that allow employees to flourish. Lean creates a dramatically new environment that helps lower stress, resulting in a more healthy and productive workplace.

Let's look at selected Lean principles, methods (processes), and tools to see how they deliver positive health benefits for all employees:

"Continuous Improvement" Principle

Despite the appearance of being adaptive, most organizations are largely status-quo oriented. When "improvement" does occur, it often happens through expensive, periodic initiatives. Or, by spending a lot of money on new technology. Management's complacency forces them to have to cram change into the organization on short notice, frequently accompanied by reorganizations and layoffs. This disruptive, often multi-year process puts tremendous mental and physical stress on employees at all levels, as roles and responsibilities rapidly change. The sense of a loss of control over one's future induces fear and anxiety. And, the changes that are eventually made invariably fall short of expectations.

In contrast, daily, incremental continuous improvement, with a mindset to "spend ideas instead of spending dollars," places less stress on people. It recognizes that most people have an innate desire to improve their work, and that it is better to do so in small ways over time rather than in a big way all at once. Through repetitive learning cycles, employees become better at identifying and correcting problems, and also avoiding problems from the start. They have responsibility for their work and the authority to improve it. Employees feel good about being in control and achieving favorable outcomes.

Expecting people to change processes a little over time is far more sensible and realistic than expecting people to change a lot all at once. The necessary changes get made in real-time, rather than having to be batched into a future major initiative. Thus, daily continuous improvement has a more positive impact on human health in the workplace.

"Respect for People" Principle

Employees who are treated disrespectfully by their management will spend a lot of time wondering what is wrong with them. Whatever the mode of disrespect, employees will be preoccupied with their own shortcomings and by future demonstrations of disrespect from managers. Disrespecting employees – treating them as a number (disposable), as nothing more than labor (vs. brains), or as a cost – shifts their attention from work to the ways in which they have been devalued.

What would you rather have employees focus on: a low sense of self-worth, or their work and how to improve it?

Managers that do not treat employees with respect introduce a source of stress that need not exist to begin with. Importantly, disrespecting employees blocks the flow of information and makes it impossible to realize daily continuous improvement. It also makes it impossible to achieve material and information flow.

Every employee wants to be treated with respect. This is the key that opens the door to continuous improvement. Employees are willing participants if they know they will be treated respectfully and in other non-zero-sum ways. They will not be receptive to learning new things in a blame-oriented environment, where they are socially and psychologically stressed by bosses. The "Respect for People" principle is not optional in Lean management.

Policy Deployment (Hoshin Kanri)

Most organizations struggle to align strategy to objectives and resources. As a result of this difficulty, organizations usually pursue too many objectives with too few resources. People waste time and energy working on things that are not very important. Invariably, much less is accomplished that was desired. At performance appraisal time, employees are criticized (blamed) for having failed to achieve their goal(s).

Policy deployment, also known as "strategy deployment," is a rigorous process for avoiding such outcomes. It connects corporate strategy to the daily work of individuals in every department, and thus aligns key objectives with available resources. The benefits of policy deployment are wide-ranging. Employees at all levels know exactly what they should be working on and how it connects to the company's objectives and strategy. The work that employees do is challenging but achievable, and variances are subject to problem-solving (PDCA) that is focused on correcting process problems and not on blaming people. Hence, failure to achieve objectives becomes a process problem and not a people problem.

The correct use of policy deployment makes work more clear, focused, fact-based, and rewarding. Everyone clearly understands the "what" and the "how," which aligns the organization and promotes teamwork. Employees are far less preoccupied about failure or the consequences of failure, thereby removing major sources of stress from their daily work lives.

Kaizen

Problem recognition in most organizations is not fact-based. It is often colored by organizational politics and other perceptions meant to minimize the size or extent of the problem. Problem-solving tends to be ad hoc and address symptoms rather than root causes. In short, employees and managers misunderstand the true problem and guess at solutions. There is no systematic process for improvement. As a result, problems are likely to recur. The normal thing to do under such circumstances is to blame people for problems and their recurrence.

Kaizen is the application of the Scientific Method to problem-solving in organizations. It teaches employees and managers how to recognize problems, analyze problems, identify and implement practical countermeasures to prevent recurrence, and measure and evaluate results. And, it teaches them how to do this quickly. The three principles of kaizen help assure that the focus is on the process that is generating the problem, and not on the people.

Kaizen, done right, gives employees more involvement and say in what they do, and a sense of reward for their efforts. It humanizes the workplace and improves cross-functional teamwork, communication, and enthusiasm for work. Kaizen creates a better social environment and temporarily erases hierarchies. It promotes social affiliation and helps leaders to better understand the work that employees do (and vice versa, where employees participate in kaizen for managerial processes). Kaizen results in improved processes by eliminating waste, unevenness, and unreasonableness. More reliable processes lower the stress on both managers and employees.

Just-In-Time (JIT)

Processing of material and information in batch-and-queue organizations is partially or completely asynchronous. That means that processing is intermittent as a result of lengthy queues, delays (such as shortages or set-ups), the time needed to transport, re-work, changing priorities, and so on. These companies are forced to perpetually run their business in a just-in-case mode because there is little control or predictability in any process. This "push" production system is a chaotic, expensive, and error-prone way to do business, and invariably leads to dissatisfied customers. (By "production," I mean any productive activity that creates value or which supports value creation).

The Just-in-Time system of production seeks to provide exactly what is needed, when it is needed, in the amount needed, to the place(s) it is needed (using kanban). It is a "pull" production system paced by the average rate of customer demand and that relies on upstream signaling to provide work instructions. This eliminates the need for centralized control of production, as is characteristically found in batch-and-queue processing.

JIT, done right, seeks to achieve synchronous coupling of internal and external processes (and demand with supply), and do so in a way that is reliable and repeatable. It gives employees a sense of control and predictability (a rhythm), which is responsive to the natural way that humans like to do work.

Autonomation (Jidoka)

In normal batch-and-queue processing, people and processes produce outputs, usually at high speed, that may or may not conform to quality requirements. Defective work is pushed to the process downstream where the next person in line has to contend with quality problems. The defective work then sits in queue before being sent back upstream for credit or for re-work. Someone will surely get blamed for this problem.

Autonomation means "automation with a human touch." It provides workers and machines with the capability to detect errors as soon as they happen. Immediately upon the detection of errors, work is stopped and problem-solving routines begin. In this way, processes do not produce both good and bad quality items, as is the case with batch-and-queue, which are then consumed in subsequent processes.

Autonomation, like most Lean methods and tools, helps people focus on the process, with facts and data, rather than blaming each other for mistakes.

Level-Loading (Heijunka)

As an asynchronous processing method, batch-and-queue is unconcerned about what work to do when. The order and sequence of work are all jumbled all the time. How can people consistently succeed under such highly variable conditions?

In Lean management, leveling the workload over a fixed period of time helps achieve basic stability, and is the foundation for success in doing value-creating work. A Just-in-Time system cannot function properly without level loading. Leveling the type and quantity of work helps to avoid batching and demand amplification ("bullwhip effect"), and offers numerous financial and non-financial benefits.

From the workers' perspective, it is absolutely clear to them what they need to do. They can do their jobs better because they are not confused about what to work on. Leveling workloads helps assure that employees output (supply) is closely coupled to actual customer demand (internal or external customer). There is a measure of control and predictability that eases mental burdens that would otherwise be placed on workers.

Takt Time

Organizations that process material and information via batch-and-queue tend to rely on sales forecasts to determine what to produce on a daily basis. Invariably, they over-produce stuff that does not sell, and under-produce stuff that is selling well. The inventory and missed sales opportunities lead senior managers to do what is easiest for them to do: blame people for these problems. Employees, unable to predict the future, are blamed by managers for failing to predict the future. The outcome: heads roll.

Takt time is the rate of customer demand. It is like the beat or tempo in music. It sets the pace of an activity. It is used in Lean management to help ensure that processes are able to produce at or near the rate of customer demand (by eliminating waste, unevennesss, and unreasonableness), thereby avoiding shortages and surpluses. Takt time directly connects workers to the marketplace. It tells them exactly what is wanted, when it is wanted, and in what quantities. No guesswork. Takt times gives people a tangible sense of control and predictability, which, of course, lowers stress.

Standardized Work

Most organizations have some form of work instructions for employees to guide their work and help them avoid errors. Often, the work instructions are complicated and difficult to understand, resulting in errors and re-work.

Lean management makes use of standardized work and standardized work combination sheets. Their purpose is multi-fold: to clarify and simplify the work done in a process, and make the work explicit so that other people can do the work (provided they receive some basic training). Standardized work helps avoid errors and maintain productivity, quality, and safety.

It makes abnormal conditions visible to that they can be quickly recognized and corrected.

Standardized work is the foundation upon which improvements are made and sustained. Improvements (kaizen) cannot take place without standardized work, both for the type of work that employees do and the type of work that managers do.

Standardized work sets people up to succeed. It helps to avoid the kinds of problems in the workplace that cause managers to blame employees (and other managers).

Set-Up Reduction

It remains common today to find companies that still have single- or multi-hour changeover times; i.e. the time between the last item completed and the first good item produced. The process is not producing goods or services during changeovers. Hours worth of output are lost, which increases costs and places pressure on people to speed-up and catch-up (assuming sales are robust). And, because forecasts are often wrong, workers must frequently switch between items produced, resulting in significant productive time lost to changeovers. This creates a chronically stressful environment of firefighting and expediting.

In Lean management, changeover times are reduced to 9 minutes or less. This has a great impact on productive capacity, increasing output 50-500 percent without any additional resources. It allows the company to produce more (assuming there is actual demand). Reducing set-up time is important for other reasons as well. It reduces burdens on employees and makes set-ups easier for them to perform. It also results in less scrap and re-work, and faster responsiveness to changes in customer demand.

Set-up reduction removes incentives for managers to make work more stressful by speeding employees up or yelling at them for being behind in their work (or for doing the wrong things).

Flow (One-Piece Flow)

Batch-and-queue processing is commonly found in organizations that use sales forecasts to drive daily execution. Both batch-and-queue processing and forecasts create numerous problems that make it nearly impossible for people to succeed consistently. Commitment to these methods assures that management prefers the status quo and is indifferent to the daily frustrations and difficulties that employees face in doing their jobs.

Flow is the opposite of batch-and-queue processing. The latter hides problems, and thus makes improving difficult. Flow makes problems visible and triggers immediate improvement in real time. Thus, problems are less likely to linger and go uncorrected. The firefighting, expediting, and blame that accompany mismatches in supply and demand with batch-and-queue are greatly reduced with one-piece flow. The timing and synchronization that is required to achieve one-piece (and continuous) flow assures better quality and shorter lead-times, which once again help avoid firefighting, expediting, and blame.

Material and Information Flow Diagrams

Batch-and-queue processing is normally depicted using traditional business process mapping diagrams (flow charts). They succeed at documenting the process activities, sequence, and decision points, but lack detailed information that would provide people with specific direction for improvement. As a result, batch-and-queue process are locally optimized, usually at someone else expense (upstream or downstream), or not improved at all.

Material and information flow diagrams (popularly known as value stream maps) are data-rich depictions of material and information flow that are used to help people understand the current state of a process and identify opportunities for improvement to achieve a desired future state. Material and information flow diagrams help assure people's efforts are focused on making improvements that achieve flow, for production processes or for management processes.

Material and information flow diagrams help employees understand what is going on, from order to delivery, and put them in control of determining where to improve the process using kaizen. Knowing what is going on and having the ability to identify and make changes for the better gives people a sense of control and a feeling of accomplishment.

5S (Sort, Straighten, Shine, Standardize, Sustain)

Workplaces in which batch-and-queue processing takes place are normally dirty or disorganized. People are so busy fighting fires that they have no time to clean and organize their workplace.

Because the workplaces in which batch-and-queue processing takes place are normally dirty or disorganized, people have great difficulty finding the things they need to do their jobs. They engage in frustrating and time-consuming searches for necessary items or information, and are thus unable to do their jobs. The resulting loss of productivity usually means someone is going to get blamed.

Lean management recognizes that dirty and disorganized workplaces lead to quality problems, work problems, poor morale, and a lack of pride in work. 5S corrects these problems and enables the establishment of a visual workplace that makes it easier for workers to understand what is going on and when abnormal conditions arise. Like all other Lean processes and tools, this reduces confusion and uncertainty.

Visual Workplace

In batch-and-queue businesses, their processes, condition, and performance are usually difficult to discern because processing steps are decoupled and asynchronous. Performance is often tracked by information systems whose data may not be readily visible to those doing the work. As a result, the system is not well understood and response to problems are usually delayed.

In Lean management, the processes, their condition, and performance are presented visually, rather than being embedded in computer systems. Andon lights, production display boards, mistake-proofing devices, supermarkets, etc., give workers instant information about the status of work. This reduces confusion and uncertainty, and enables employees to respond rapidly to abnormal conditions when they occur.

A3 Reports

As mentioned previously, problem-solving in batch-and-queue environments tends to be ad hoc and reactionary. The use of problem-solving methods and tools is inconsistent. People guess at the causes of problems, which leads to inaccurate or ineffective solutions. Telling managers that a problem is "solved" (i.e. the symptom has been identified and corrected) is often more important than actually solving the problem. As should be expected, the same problems will be repeated and consume resources again and again. Someone is going to pay… A3 reports are a structured problem solving process. A problem is analyzed completely within the confines of one side of an A3 sized sheet of paper (11 x 17 inches). It includes the current condition, target condition, root cause analysis, countermeasures, implementation plan, and criteria for evaluating results.

Through repeated use of A3 reports, employees (and senior managers) improve their abilities to identify and correct problems (vs. repeating problems). Workers and managers develop a valuable skill that helps them understand processes and how to improve them, rather than blame people for problems.

Root Cause Analysis

Managers in most organizations talk about the root cause of this or that problem, but they never actually do any root cause analysis. In every graduate-level course that I have taught since 1999, I have asked my students if they have ever seen root cause analysis (5 Whys or fishbone diagram) from someone at a vice president level or above. The answer is always the same: "No." This is true even in organizations that have root cause analysis as an integral part of their operating system.

The message that this sends to employees is unmistakable: "We leaders do not have problems," or "Our problems are of a nature that cannot be solved using root cause analysis." Bullshit! Effective Lean leaders recognize that they will not be credible if they do not do the same things that they ask of followers. People at all levels have problems, and they must use the same problem solving processes [19]. The health benefit of using A3 reports and of root cause analysis is to remove uncertainty as to the cause of problems, and gives employees confidence that they can eliminate errors or reduce their frequency of occurrence. Root cause analysis becomes easier to do with practice and gives people comfort in that they understand what is going on. They are not perplexed by process or system variation, and can then make good decisions.

Quality Function Deployment (QFD)

The design of products and services tends to be driven by engineers whose perspectives of good design and functionality are often at odds with how customers perceive good design and functionality. Money invested in design and production is often difficult to recover because the product or service has missed the market. Inventories build and discounts are offered to move the merchandise. Because things did not go according to plan, people have to explain what went wrong and report on cost and schedule variances. The opportunities to blame people for making mistakes are endless.

To help avoid such outcomes, Lean businesses use the Quality Function Deployment process to assure that customers' wants and needs (the voice of the customer) are incorporated into the engineering design and specifications for the product or service. QFD greatly reduces the chances that the product or service will fail in the marketplace. Successful products and services mitigate any need for managers to get upset with people. This is how QFD delivers a positive health benefit to employees.

Cells (Work Cells)
Work is normally done in islands in batch-and-queue processing. Subsequent processing steps are located some distance away – far enough so that the people doing the processing do not interact with each other. Workers, driven by their supervisors, toil away independently of upstream or downstream processes. They overproduce, they under-produce. They produce good quality and they produce defectives. The system is asynchronous and unbalanced, and therefore prone to failure, firefighting, and blame.

In Lean, the people that do the processing are located in close proximity to one another so that they can get to know each other and work together to identify problems and improve their processes. People and processes are arranged in the sequence in which value is added, usually in U-shaped work cells. The system is synchronous and balanced, and therefore operates with much higher reliability, while the incentives to blame people for problems are greatly diminished.

Mistake-Proofing
In most workplaces, problems and errors are bad things that people try to keep hidden because they fear the consequences. However, you cannot improve if you don't know about problems. Yet, in batch-and-queue environments, employees and managers prefer to ignore problems. In addition, little is done to give employees awareness of what mistakes look like and how to prevent them. As a result, improvement is intermittent and painfully slow.

In Lean management, problems are good because they tell people exactly what to work on. Problems help drive continuous improvement when people are not blamed for mistakes. Continuous improvement also involves efforts to prevent mistakes and errors from occurring to begin with. Teams quickly study a problem and create simple, low cost devices to prevent errors. These mistake-proofing devices deliver greater process control and predictability. Everyone is happier in workplaces that experience fewer errors and high process reliability – and more satisfied knowing that they helped make that happen.

Yokoten (Sharing)

Batch-and-queue environments tend to be hyper-competitive among employees, in part to dodge problems. Nobody wants a big problem to stick to them. Knowledge is seen as a great source of power and job security, and therefore people are loathe to share ideas (or any other resource) with one another. People hoard information and release it to others only when necessary. Information does not flow. People cannot easily get the information they need to do their jobs.

Lean organizations apply the concept of "yokoten," which means to deploy (or copy) good results (and good thinking) horizontally across the company – to share ideas, concepts, practices, policies, etc., with colleagues. Yokoten is the open sharing of successes and failures, to help others learn. It helps other employees eliminate problems that are the same or similar. Yokoten improves communication and information flow, in the spirit of helping each another. Knowing that useful information and valuable help are readily available reduces stress and improves the work experience for everyone.

• • • • •

I have presented 20 examples of Lean principles, methods, and tools that deliver positive health benefits to the employees in organizations that understand and practice Lean management well. While this is not a complete list, you will find that other methods and tools deliver similar positive health benefits to all employees in an organization.

Lean is a smartly designed management system that executives, professors, and other influential people have misunderstood or ignored for far too long. Importantly, these same Lean principles, methods (processes) and tools can be used to correct the leadership process problems cited in Lesson 57.

However, Lean principles, methods and tools alone mean nothing. They must be brought to life by people – especially senior managers – through daily application to create a new environment. Healthcare is everywhere in Lean management, when it is done right.

I will never forget interviewing executives of The Wiremold Company when doing research for the book *Better Thinking, Better Results.* I had never seen calmer senior managers. It paralleled what I experienced with my boss when I was first learning about Lean in the mid-1990s, and what I have seen since then in organizations that practice Lean well. A Lean environment is not utopia by any means, and there are many instances of acute stress. However, chronic stress is reduced by the design of the system and in its correct practice.

Given what I have seen of executives who understood and practiced Lean well (calm demeanor, process-focused, effective problem-solvers, etc.), my questions to senior managers who remain committed to batch-and-queue processing are: Don't you want to have a better life at work? How can you be satisfied with your own work, when you have so little sense of control and predictability? How can you be satisfied that employees have so little sense of control and predictability? Why do you keep working in ways that make life so difficult for everyone? Why don't you set people up to succeed? Don't you want to improve the health and well-being of all employees?

Senior managers have to adopt Lean management in its entirety obtain the health benefits. They cannot pick and choose which Lean principles, processes, and tools to use and which to ignore. If they do so, they will create a hybrid batch-and-queue/Lean system that will increase chronic stress in the organization.

The workplace will always be unhealthy when Lean is misunderstood and misapplied. Healthharm is everywhere in Lean management when it is practiced incorrectly.

Lesson 68

Don't Be a Stress Raiser

One of the things that young mechanical and civil engineers learn about early in their education is stress concentrations. A stress concentration is a geometric feature or discontinuity in an object that locally concentrates stress to higher levels than the surrounding region. Stress concentrations, also known as stress raisers or stress risers, can cause small cracks to form. Over time, the cracks may grow and eventually lead to failure of a component or structure. The failure may be small and simply annoying (e.g. a broken handle), or it can be large and severe and cause injury or death to many people (e.g. a bridge collapse).

The image below illustrates a stress concentration caused by the presence of a small round hole in a large metal plate.

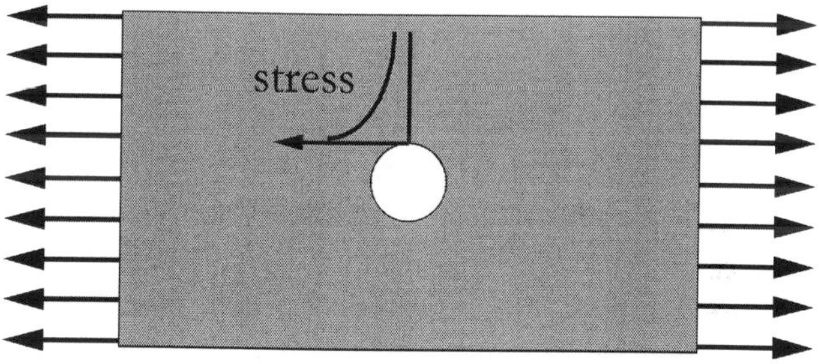

In the absence of the hole, the plate would experience a uniform stress due to the load placed on it, as indicated by the arrows at the ends of the plate. The presence of a hole raises the stress in the region of the plate that is closest to the hole. Often, stress raisers are not uniform in shape, such as a perfectly round hole. They can be irregular, such as an ellipse or sharp wedge-shaped crack, where the stress at the crack tip will be highly concentrated – usually to well beyond the strength of the material that the plate is made of. This type of stress raiser is of great concern to engineers because the crack may grow very rapidly and cause sudden failure. Hence, the use of safety factors in the design of load-bearing structures.

If an engineer wants something to work reliably for a long time, they have to recognize and manage all stress concentrations in the design. Engineers seek to identify and reduce or eliminate stress raisers, to remove them as a possible mode of failure. The reason why buildings do not fall down, why airplanes don't fall out of the sky, and why your car runs properly is because engineers, over time, have done an good job of understanding materials and managing micro and macro stress concentrations. Components and structures function according to plan and last a long time. The people that use them are not inconvenienced by failures. Therefore, they are happy.

Yet, even well designed components and structures are subject to different types of periodic inspections to assure that they do not fail prematurely. Failure, if inevitable, must be controlled and not sudden or catastrophic. In this way, small problems are managed or corrected before they turn into big problems. Sometimes, failure is sudden and catastrophic, which leads to a thorough engineering failure analysis to determine the specific mode(s) of failure. The results of such investigations are incorporated into future designs to eliminate repeat failures. In this way, engineers avoid chronic failures and can instead focus on acute failures. Overall, engineers do a very good job of learning from failures.

Like an engineered component or structure, organizations are also designed by people. The organizational design – including its many processes – may be haphazard or well thought-out. The design may be good enough to get the job done, though error-prone, or it might instead be highly reliable. Either way, someone thought about the known requirements and created a design that they felt would function adequately – but invariably *without* consideration of safety factors.

Organizational design is usually hierarchical, as organization charts illustrate. Hierarchies, however, typically result in many abnormal conditions related to information flow. In addition, most of the processes needed to run a business and to satisfy customers are batch-and-queue. That means material and information flow are interrupted often, typically for long durations, for myriad reasons. As a result, most organizations are designed to have numerous recurring abnormal conditions. They are designed-in, which is why so many problems seem to be intractable (hence, people say, "Get used to it; that's just the way things are").

Furthermore, organizations are usually not very good at determining the causes of abnormal conditions at the source – the root causes. Instead, they focus on symptoms and devise temporary fixes, which in most cases is good enough for the organization's leaders. This reflects the type of superficial education that most managers receive with respect to problem-solving. Unfortunately, the same problems are sure to be repeated due to inattention to the root cause(s) of failure. Overall, managers do a very poor job of learning from the many failures that they experience.

Problems – actually, abnormal conditions – are the organizational equivalent of stress raisers in engineering. They are technical or behavioral discontinuities that locally concentrate stress to much higher levels than the surrounding region. Hierarchies and batch-and-queue processing is an organizational design that is awash in stress raisers. Unlike in engineering, in business most managers ignore the presence of stress raisers and even increase the number of stress raisers (e.g. by increasing the number of metrics, overloading people with work, unrealistic deadlines, etc.). They inadvertently design organizations that are prone to failure. People affected by hierarchies and batch-and-queue processing are inconvenienced by these failures. Therefore, they are unhappy.

The image below illustrates a process that is functioning according to plan. There is a uniform stress due to the load placed on the process as it runs (arrows).

The image below illustrates an abnormal condition that has occurred in the process. The presence of a hole (the abnormal condition) raises the stress in the region of the process that is closest to the abnormal condition. The abnormal condition, for example, is one that keeps an internal or external customer waiting or otherwise results in a noticeable inconvenience.

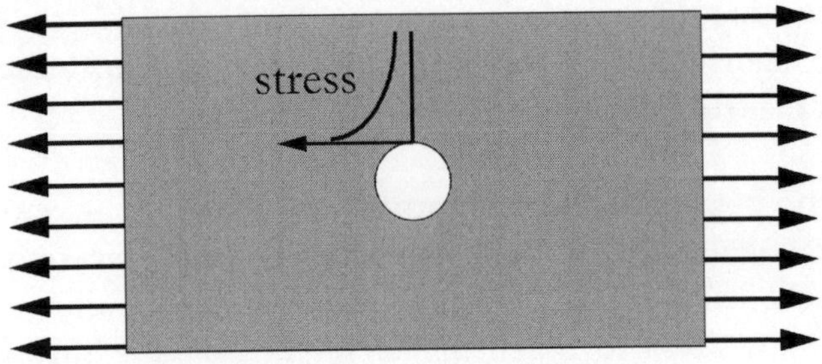

The people managing the process are likely aware of the abnormal condition and may or may not correct it without management intervention.

However, abnormal conditions often get the attention of managers, whose behaviors can be aggressive or disrespectful when they intervene. Their involvement can quickly change the shape of the stress raiser from circular to star-shaped, where the stress at the tips of the star is intensified – often well beyond the ability (strength) of the people to manage the stress. The next image depicts this type of stress raiser, which should be of great concern to managers because it will reduce teamwork, creativity, and innovation, and, if it persists, will lead to worker burn-out (failure).

Hierarchies and batch-and-queue processing means, by definition, that managers will be far more results-focused than process-focused. The most common reaction to abnormal conditions by managers is to blame people. Blame turns a small problem into a bigger problem by cutting off the flow of information. Chronic problems lead to chronic blame and information flow problems, which leads to chronic stress in people. Managers' contribution to stress concentration can be significant, sometimes much greater than the problem itself (e.g. when they make a mountain out of a molehill).

The image below depicts a hierarchical organization that processes material and information batch-and-queue. It has an abundance of technical (process) behavioral (blame, etc.) stress raisers occurring at any given point in time. The steady-state condition of such an organization is numerous abnormal conditions all the time, many of them hidden because people fear the consequences of speaking up.

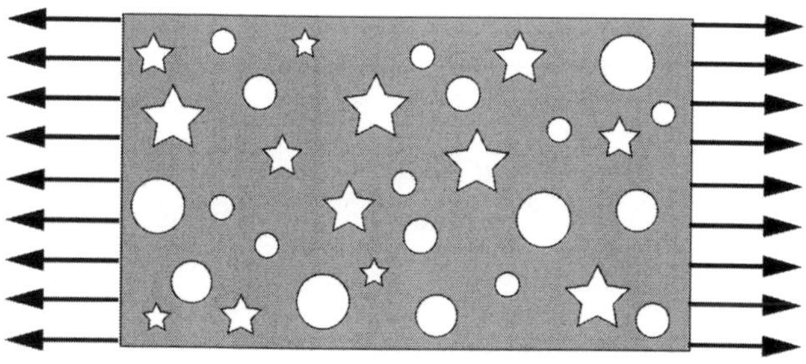

As might be expected, workers are frustrated. Managers are frustrated. And customers are unhappy.

The organization has so many process and leadership behavior problems occurring simultaneously that they weaken the organization, much like the perforations in a sheet of postage stamps weakens the paper they are printed on. The probability of a large, expensive, and embarrassing failure is very high, with such failures typically occurring every 10 years or so.

A question you may ask is, "Why doesn't the organization fail more often?" Actually, it is failing all the time, but people react quickly to crises and heroes save the day. The hero is rewarded while others are ignored or penalized. Also, money hides problems. You may observe, "The organization is successful; it does not seem like it is failing." It might not be failing, but it is weakening, and will suffer significant failures under the right conditions. The point is that management should not do things to create, accentuate, or perpetuate weakness. They should eliminate the types of stress raisers that are known to cause failures.

New leaders typically inherit an organization's design, including all of its faulty processes. They often "improve" things by changing the organization chart and some key business processes – yet most of the technical and behavioral stress raisers remain. Stress raisers, abundant and ever-present, assure that the organization, while looking as if it is performing well, is actually underperforming.

Leaders must instead lead efforts to understand the various types of technical and behavioral stress raisers, and then redesign the organization and its processes to reduce or eliminate stress raisers. Concurrently, leaders must adopt new leadership behaviors that are consistent with the new organizational and process designs to reduce or eliminate stress raisers. This is what Lean management can help an organization do better than any other system of management. However, even well-designed Lean organizations and their processes are subject to different types of periodic inspections to assure that they do not fail prematurely or catastrophically. As a result, major failures are typically fewer in number and occur less frequently.

Organizations have naturally occurring stresses due to hierarchies, budgets, processes, new technology, competition, etc. The concern is when stress raisers go unrecognized or are allowed by leaders to proliferate and create chronically stressful work environments for people.

Such problems are not free, yet most managers act as if they are. Dealing with the same problem over and over again is a drain on all the various types of resources available to an organization, which creates resource stress raisers. Hence, people often say, "We don't have the resources to do that." With Lean management, resources are created when stress raisers are diminished.

In engineering, managing stress raisers leads to longer life components and structures. In business, managing stress raisers leads to longer life in people at work. So, as a leader, what should you learn how to do?

Closing Remarks

I would like conclude by reminding readers that they must always be optimistic about progressive Lean management, despite many difficult challenges. However, difficult challenges should not be equated with drudgery. Far from it. Lean management, done right, is so much fun for everyone.

The changes in the way leaders see things, think about things, and do things are liberating for followers as well as for leaders. People, for the first time, begin to have fun at work. When people have fun, work transforms from simply a paycheck to something much greater: realizing human potential.

The boss's commitment, sense of curiosity, and passion for improvement drives followers to learn even more and to continue deepening their understanding of Lean management. The documentary movie *Jiro Dreams of Sushi* and the PBS television show *The Mind of a Chef* illustrate the fun that these people have in their endless pursuit of improvement. To them, difficult challenges are the only challenges worthy of their precious time on earth.

Your time on earth is precious too. What will you do with it?

Everything presented in this book is sensible, practical, and achievable. Rather than generating wide-ranging abnormal conditions and being satisfied with that, senior managers should become highly motivated to learn what the normal condition is for all processes and strive to achieve that. This will challenge senior managers to think about employees and their roles and responsibilities in business. In particular, whether or not people are the problem, and their value when it comes to problem avoidance, problem-solving, creativity, and innovation.

It should also challenge executives who complain about the cost of healthcare to see connections between how they lead and how they manage day-to-day business activities in relation to their effect on the health of employees. Executives grumble about the cost of medical tests, pharmaceuticals, and so on, but fail to correlate the tests and medications prescribed to employees and dysfunctional leadership and wasteful organizational behaviors.

Workers are generally viewed by executives, either explicitly or implicitly, as a threat or enemy that impairs the ability of the company to achieve growth targets and year-over-year improvement in financial performance. Biases and stereotypes, perhaps largely unconscious (and thus, implicit), have the effect of diminishing workers and converting them into sub-human actors whose fate is determined by executive whim. Hence, the brutal terms used to describe layoffs: "cut heads," "terminate," "get axed," "slash headcount," etc.

While executive's view of workers comes and goes over time, this negative view seems to be especially strong in recent decades – despite the fact that they are often severely mismanaged.

This book also challenges leaders to make work fun, because doing so has a positive benefit on human health in the form of reduced stress among both managers and employees. Human happiness must be part of work, not separate from it.

Improving the way executives lead, inclusive of the management system used, for the benefit of improved human health is not solely a matter of benevolence towards employees. It is also rooted in the hard facts of competitive business: The unyielding need for cost reduction and the need for people to create and innovate in order to improve the value proposition for customers.

I hope that I have convinced you that people are not the problem; that it is OK to hire people and to pay them well. One hundred years ago, Frederick Winslow Taylor argued strenuously that wages can be high and costs can be low concurrently. Executives rarely comprehend this fact. In addition, managers must systematically coach and develop employees' capabilities and focus on processes and how to improve them in order to achieve desired business results in relation to customer wants and needs.

Human health in organizations cannot be improved by continuing to lead and manage in the same tired ways. I am hopeful you will adopt the positive perspective that senior managers are the physicians of business and they must do no harm to employees or other stakeholders. You will have to learn many new things to serve effectively in this role. Despite decades of business experience, you should consider yourself as a first-year student.

While it would be wonderful to instantly have great Lean leadership at the top of an organization, that is usually not the case. We cannot wait for someone else high above us in the organization to finally "get it." Instead, we must move forward as best we can. There is so much that you can do, on your own and as a team, to improve processes and create better outcomes for your customers, yourself, and other stakeholders.

In my current job, I work under the same constraints as most readers. My leaders do not know or care about Lean management. That does not stop me from applying Lean principles and practices to my work as a teacher. I continue to practice Lean daily and have experienced clear and substantial benefits for myself as well as my stakeholders.

This outcome is extremely rewarding and helps fuel my passion for Lean. In addition, my daily practice deepens my knowledge of Lean and prepares me for the day when I can make a greater impact. I hope you will adopt the same attitude. You may have to go about your improvement work quietly so as not to upset your peer group or senior managers. Ultimately, it is your devotion to daily improvement that matters most, not approval from peers and bosses.

I hope you have learned that Lean is not mean; that managers must not cause human suffering. They can lead and manage organizations in ways that are better for their business and also better for the health of all employees – themselves included. Happy relationships between managers and workers are healthy relationships. Leaders must humanize the workplace.

Managers and workers are a community with a shared purpose. Do not separate yourself from workers, and do not isolate workers from each other. The better leaders and managers do not dominate or oppress subordinates. Instead, they appreciate them and give them opportunities to contribute and allow their voices to be heard. Give, rather than receive. Serve others. Listen and respond to feedback. Do the work required to become a complete leader – a professional leader.

Lean management is not perfect. It will not deliver utopian work environments, perfect processes, or perfect business results. What it can do is put the focus on processes and on facts, not on people and politics. Lean removes incentives for managers to blame people for abnormal conditions and to treat people disrespectfully. That, in turn, opens the door to continuous improvement. The result is high fidelity information flows that enable more timely and better decision-making.

Finally, I hope you found this book to be both educational and inspiring, and that you are energized to correctly apply Lean principles and practices every day.

Good luck!

Appendix I

My Lean Adventure

I am often asked how I got started with Lean. My story is similar to that of many others, but differs in one crucial aspect. My on-the-job Lean training with Shingijutsu consultants made me realize very quickly that our leaders had been complacent for decades and almost every senior manager did not understand how to lead the company's Lean transformation – and still does not, more than 20 years later.

That experience led me to focus my efforts on understanding Lean leadership and developing practical ways for managers to become better leaders. The focus of my work has been to help executives recognize Lean as a non-zero-sum (win-win) management system and the importance of the "Respect for People" principle. Ultimately, my vision is to improve the health and well-being of people in organizations through Lean management.

• • • • •

My first exposure to progressive Lean management was in 1992 or 1993, when I read Masaaki Imai's book *Kaizen*. I found it interesting, but a bit difficult to relate to because I did not think in terms of processes. My attitude was, "Don't worry too much about how you do it, just get it done." I had spent the prior seven years working in engineering, mainly on various far-out research and development projects, but was growing restless and wanted to work on current products. I had always been a practical, hands-on, technical guy (I built my first racing bicycle frame at the age of 18), but somehow wound up doing R&D work whose payoff would be far into the future.

My company's manufacturing operations leadership was looking to upgrade and diversify its management team, so I interviewed for a job as a business unit manager responsible for the production of high-temperature composite parts for gas turbine engines. I got the job in July 1994 and immediately went from the serene world of engineering to the tumult of operations. I was suddenly immersed in the day-to-day challenge of producing difficult-to-make goods to an unforgiving schedule, with myriad cost, delivery, and quality problems. Thank goodness consultants from Shingijutsu were nearby.

My company had hired Shingijutsu two years earlier, and several of their kaizen consultants were busy working throughout our manufacturing operations teaching people how to improve processes using Toyota production system principles and methods. Their focus at that time was our large manufacturing facilities. The place I went to work at was a much smaller facility, which had recently come under the leadership of a general manager who was devoted to kaizen. So he arranged for Shingijutsu to come to our facility for several weeks per year shortly before I arrived.

My on-the-job Lean training with Shingijutsu began in August of 1994, in collaboration with our office of continuous improvement. Those first kaizens were eye-opening. People with a great amount of work experience and solid formal education had inadvertently created processes that consumed the maximum amount of resources possible. The batch-and-queue processes they created did indeed work – but usually only the last week of the month, and also caused unending cost, delivery, lead-time, and quality problems. So, we did kaizen; lots of kaizen.

Shingijutsu taught us how to improve both processes and teamwork. I am immensely grateful for what they taught me, but also upset that our leaders who, for so many decades prior, were comfortable and satisfied with the status-quo – batch-and-queue processing. They were also satisfied with all the overt and covert blame and finger-pointing that invariably comes with error-prone processes, and taught us how to conform and to accept chaos. As leaders, they should have taught us how to improve processes and achieve flow before we became engulfed in crisis (a problem that has recurred again today). There was plenty of published information to help with that, even if some of it was decades old – the principles and practices needed for flow are unchanging.

Kaizen was a life-altering experience for me. But it did not have that effect on most other managers. I wondered why they were so much less affected than me. Was it because I was new or because I was from engineering, while they were long-time operations people? Or, was it because they were more concerned about making their monthly batch-and-queue based metrics, and that mattered most to them?

I observed that a few of my peer-group managers led people in ways that were more consistent with Lean principles and practices. Their beliefs, behaviors, and competencies were better aligned with Lean, while other managers' beliefs, behaviors, and competencies remained aligned with batch-and-queue. I wanted to know why most managers adhered to error-prone batch-and-queue thinking and tolerated its numerous shortcomings. Why were they so comfortable with that?

In the late 1990s, I decided to devote myself to the study of Lean leadership. This was motivated by my own practice of Lean leadership beginning in 1994, from which I formulated new constructs for the daily practice of Lean leadership called "Continuous Personal Improvement" and "Lean Behaviors" (where I introduced the critically important concept of "behavioral waste" - the eighth waste). Published in 1998, these groundbreaking papers established the fundamental basis for Lean leadership.

I left industry in 1999 and joined academia, which gave me more time to study and write about Lean leadership. Nobody was researching Lean leadership in the late 1990s. It was not until 2007 that the wider Lean community began to realize its importance. Joining academia also gave me the opportunity to break new ground by applying Lean principles and practices in higher education – to my own courses and to academic programs, and teach Lean management to university administrators and Lean teaching to faculty.

Since then, I numerous books and papers, expanding on my original ideas and adding many new ones. One of my main objectives was to understand why leading a Lean business is so difficult for most senior managers. Enormous progress has been made on this front. Another objective was to make Lean leadership easier for senior managers to grasp and therefore enable daily practice. Enormous progress has been made on this as well.

I always try to produce creative and innovate work to help people who struggle with Lean leadership. It has resulted in a significantly better understanding of Lean leadership today compared to 20 years ago. But, there remains more to do.

Appendix II

Early History of Lean at Pratt & Whitney

I joined Pratt & Whitney (P&W), a division of United Technologies Corporation (UTC), in early 1988 after completing my Ph.D. in materials engineering at Brown University. After working in engineering for six years, I transferred to manufacturing operations where I had my first hands-on experience with the Toyota Production System (TPS). I participated in my first kaizen in July 1994, led by consultants from Shingijutsu who had been hired two years earlier (headed by Yoskihi Iwata and Chihiro Nakao, and comprised at that time of retired industrial engineers mainly from Toyota Gosei and also from Isuzu).

Since then, United Technologies Corporation and its divisions have developed a strong focus on continuous improvement. However, they have, as most large companies, been weak on the application of the "Respect for People" principle – though, at various times there have been islands where this was not the case (and which I was fortunate enough to experience under the leadership of Lloyd Tirey at Pratt's Rocky Hill, Connecticut, facility). Despite this common defect, the introduction and development of Lean at Pratt & Whitney is historically significant, both for the State of Connecticut and as a large corporation that was an early adopter of Lean tools and methods in the aerospace industry.

The story below describes the early days of Lean at Pratt & Whitney, principally in its Connecticut operations between 1992 and 1997. This recollection constructed with the help of two people, anonymous contributors to this Appendix, who were present around the time Pratt's Office of Continuous Improvement (OCI) was established in 1992, and written to clarify my own recollection.

The first Shingijutsu kaizen was in August of 1992 at Pratt's Middletown, Connecticut, plant, facilitated by Mr. Chihiro Nakao. Pratt & Whitney's Office of Continuous Improvement was established in October 1992 under a new executive, Bob D'Amour, and was a huge step towards the Lean journey with Shingijutsu and the attempt to create the Pratt Production System. The OCI group was highly engaged with Shingijutsu, trained for and facilitated events, led the transition into cellular manufacturing, and created the "blue book" for continuous improvement methodology at P&W and all of the Lean training materials – several of which became part of the "Achieving Competitive Excellence" (ACE) package.

The OCI team, also through Shingijutsu, introduced a Lean assessment tool which was used in Operations around the mid-1990s. Bob D'Amour left P&W in February of 1996 and Dave Haddock was temporarily put in charge until Joe Pressing was named Director for a short time, and then Grace Reed assumed the group in early 1997.

Achieving Competitive Excellence was initiated at the request of Mark Coran, vice president of Operations, in June of 1996. The first ACE "pilots" were trained in August 1996 in the North Berwick facility by Tom Voss and Tom DeForge in a train-the-trainer format. Training was focused on standard work and set-up reduction. It was a combination of training and presentation skills, with each pilot presenting the material, then going to the shop to conduct a continuous improvement activity.

Mark Coran was highly involved and was driving implementation. Dave Haddock got involved and insisted that the primary focus be on Total Productive Maintenance (TPM) and 5S (sort, straighten, shine, standardize, sustain). Haddock took over leadership of the initiative and brought in Rob Roark from Development Operations (a pre-production manufacturing engineering group), and Joe Dawson from Quality. Dave, Rob, and Joe became known internally as "The Three Amigos."

ACE started as a strategy to get the hourly workforce involved more actively in the day-to-day sustainment of the kaizen. The assessment tool was originally taken from the Isuzu assessment tool, which had 10 categories, more heavily weighted towards standard work, production balancing and leveling, and of course TPM, and 5S. Of the ten categories, TPM and 5S became the critical elements of ACE upon which everyone focused at Pratt at that time.

The evolution of ACE was the fusion of two philosophies and sets of tools: "Quality First" from Yuzuru Ito, UTCs quality consultant during the 1990s, and "Flow (Productivity) First" from Taiichi Ohno, the developer of the Toyota Production System, via Shingijutsu. ACE also has other philosophical threads and tools, known collectively as "process certification" that stem from the teachings of W. Edwards Deming and from Genichi Taguchi.

Folks from Pratt & Whitney Canada visited P&W East Hartford in the March-April 1997 time-frame to learn about ACE and begin the process of implementing it there. By that time, Dave Haddock, Joe Dawson, and Rob Roark had been appointed to the newly formed "ACE office, and that office was in the process of being spun off from the OCI group later that year, reporting to the VP of Quality. The first ACE booklet was published in early 1997, and contained the following elements: 5S/visual factory, total productive maintenance, quality control process chart, process certification, mistake proofing, set-up reduction, and standard work.

An effort began in late 1997 to gain consensus among executives in UTC's divisions to adopt ACE as the corporation's system of continuous improvement. The ACE initiative was adopted by UTC in 1998, and executives of all UTC divisions agreed to adopt ACE at the launch of an internal educational program in continuous improvement called "Ito University." Additional tools and methods were added to ACE post-1997, including UTCs problem-solving process, market feedback analysis, passport system of program review, and the designation of ACE levels of achievement: bronze, silver, and gold.

My experience with ACE began was when I was a supply chain manager. I wanted to introduce ACE to the supply base at a large supplier conference that I was organizing. I called Dave Haddock to get copies of the newly-published ACE booklet to give to our first-tier machining suppliers and second-tier outside processing suppliers. He initially did not want to share the internal publication with my suppliers.

I argued in favor of doing so and eventually won. The 92 first- and second-tier suppliers who attended the conference on 5 June 1997 received P&Ws ACE booklet as well as other important information on Lean including:

- *The Machine that Changed the World* by J. Womack, D. Jones, and D. Roos
- *Lean Thinking* by J. Womack, D. Jones
- "Continuous Improvement at Pratt & Whitney," a training booklet produced by Pratt's Office of Continuous Improvement (a derivate work of Shingijutsu's training book "How to Implement Kaizen in Manufacturing")
- Productivity Press book catalog

This was the first time that Pratt's first- and second-tier suppliers were introduced to ACE on a broad basis.

The suppliers, most of whom were small, family-owned businesses, were skeptical of our intentions at the time, thinking Lean was just another way for Pratt to force them to lower prices. Most did not recognize the potential that Lean offered to help them become more responsive to changing market conditions as well as assure their own long-term survival. A few suppliers, however, recognized the opportunity and welcomed our help. Our continuous improvement engineers spent a lot of time at these suppliers, most of which are still around today (and, we must acknowledge, in large part due to their own skillful capabilities to survive despite great pressure to rapidly reduce costs, improve quality, and reduce lead-times). Though, pressure remains on Pratt's Connecticut suppliers in the form of a goal to increase by 300% the amount of work offshored to low-wage countries through 2015.

While I initially supported efforts to reduce Lean to a subset of tools taught to us by our Shingijutsu consultants, this was, in hindsight, a significant error. For many years, it perpetuated the common misunderstanding at Pratt of Lean as nothing more than tools to cut costs (inclusive of layoffs and outsourcing, as is often the case) and improve quality and productivity in operations. This was both the internal perception and the perception of other large corporations seeking to improve their operations. Thus, it greatly delayed comprehension of Lean as a comprehensive system of management, and it reduced employee involvement because the impact of Lean on them was often unfavorable.

In addition, it was detrimental for Lean to be viewed internally as, alternatingly, an "operations thing" and as a "quality thing." The periodic shifting of Lean/ACE between the operations and quality organizations caused unnecessary confusion and additional delays in the absorption of Lean principles and practices. Today, UTC associates ACE with quality and the quality organization, and is characterized as the means to achieve quality products and processes.

I left Pratt & Whitney in 1998 and joined UTC's corporate office in Hartford, Connecticut. I left UTC a year later and joined Rensselaer Polytechnic University, Lally School of Management and Technology (their satellite campus located in Hartford, Connecticut). A few years after that, ACE was elevated to become UTCs official operating system for all business units, and, over time, more broadly applied to each function/discipline within the divisions to varying degrees of success according to former students of mine.

Many companies, both large and small, have followed the same or similar path as UTC, beginning with Lean tools used in operations and slowly evolving them into to a corporate operating system – but not into an overall system of management for the entire enterprise (inclusive of critically important aspects such as Lean accounting). Again, in hindsight, it should have started to become apparent soon after publication in 1993 of the first edition of Yasuhiro Monden's book, *Toyota Management System*, that Lean was more than just a production system. Taiichi Ohno told us that in 1988, and Professor Monden showed us that TPS was an overall company management system, and one in which the "Respect for People" principle was of equal importance to continuous improvement.

This historical account of the early days of Lean at Pratt & Whitney is important from an educational perspective and contains three significant learning lessons:

1. How Lean tools can completely captivate individuals and corporations, and therefore make it very difficult to advance the understanding of Lean as a comprehensive, principle-based, non-zero-sum (win-win) system of management designed for competitive buyers' markets – in addition to understanding how leadership thinking and routines must change. This has been a major struggle since the beginning of progressive management in the late 1800s and early 1900s. Frederick Winslow Taylor, who created Scientific Management (and, with Frank Gilbreth, industrial engineering – the antecedent to Lean management), encountered the very same problem. They never found the solution, and neither have we.

2. Consultants' approach to teaching Lean – even the best consultants – reinforce the perception among managers and workers that Lean is nothing more than tools to use within the larger framework of an organization's existing management system. Taylor and his followers also encountered the same problem in the late 1800s and early

1900s. Once again, they never found the solution, and neither have we.

3. The inability to find solutions to these two problems over many decades suggests that progressive Lean management has stalled. While some organizations have been able to move beyond the popular representation of Lean (as tools) and achieve a more fundamental transformation in management (and employee) thinking and practice most have not. Empirical observations reveal formidable barriers to change that are often greatest among those leaders whose calls for change are the loudest.

My experience at Pratt & Whitney was positive and both personally and professionally transformative. It inspired me to do what I have done for the last 20 years: to inform Lean practitioners of the importance of the "Respect for People" principle as both the enabler and sustaining feature for employee engagement in daily continuous improvement and to rigorously teach Lean as an overall management system, for the entire enterprise. And, it is what led me to focus intensely on leadership as the defining characteristic of whether Lean transformations are successful, or whether management picks only pieces of Lean – selected tools and methods – to squeeze more juice from the lemon.

———

Special thanks to the two anonymous contributors for their help writing this Appendix (pages 310 and 311).

About the Author

M.L. "Bob" Emiliani is a professor in the School of Engineering, Science, and Technology at Connecticut State University in New Britain, Conn., where he teaches courses on Lean management and a unique course that analyzes failures in management decision-making.

Bob holds a bachelor's degree in mechanical engineering from the University of Miami, a master's degree in chemical engineering from the University of Rhode Island, and a Ph.D. degree in Engineering from Brown University.

He worked in the consumer products and aerospace industries for 15 years, beginning as a materials engineer. He has held management positions in engineering, manufacturing, and supply chain management, and had responsibility for implementing Lean in manufacturing and supply chains at Pratt & Whitney.

Bob joined academia in September 1999 at Rensselaer Polytechnic Institute (Hartford, Connecticut campus) and worked there until 2004. He has applied Lean principles and practices to the courses he teaches since he joined academia, and led the first kaizens to improve an accredited master's degree program in 2002-2003. He joined Connecticut State University in 2005.

Emiliani has authored or co-authored more than 20 books, four book chapters, over 35 peer-reviewed papers on Lean management and related topics, and 10 papers on materials science and engineering. He has received six awards for writing.

Please visit my web site www.bobemiliani.com.

11368280R00194

Printed in Great Britain
by Amazon.co.uk, Ltd.,
Marston Gate.